Never Pluck a Persimmon:

The story of a Hoosier community
the people therein,
their schools,
their fall festival,
and the persimmon, the fruit
"you dassn't pick"

By

Virginia Morrow Black

© 2002 by Virginia Morrow Black. All rights reserved.

No part of this book may be reproduced, stored in a retrieval system, or transmitted by any means, electronic, mechanical, photocopying, recording, or otherwise, without written permission from the author.

ISBN: 0-7596-5146-9

This book is printed on acid free paper.

1stBooks-rev. 1/4/02

PREFACE

"Never pluck a persimmon," is a kind of slogan in Greentree, Indiana, but it is an admonition as well.

"Don't you do it!" my brand new landlady, Mrs. Nadine Decklebaum, warned. "A plucked persimmon can pucker up your lips like they wasn't a part of you,—like an extra 'pendage," she continued, pursing her lips into an arrangement that resembled the gill-folds on the underside of a full-grown mushroom.

"You bein' a schoolteacher and all," she added, "could make you look mighty prissy! Fifty dollars a week with breakfast," Mrs. Decklebaum had changed the subject.

"I'll take it," I sealed the bargain, "but I don't quite understand about persimmons. I've never even tasted one." And with these words, I was back on Mrs. Decklebaum's merry-go-round.

For the next hour, then, I was briefed concerning these plumlike oblate spheres around which the entire town of Greentree gyrated. Persimmons, I discovered, were powerful important to the people of this tiny Hoosier community. Because the wild persimmon tree favors the soil and climate of few areas in the United States, Greentree-ers, I learned, considered themselves 'specially blessed.

To make use of these resources, then, Greentree had its own Persimmon Planning Committee which resurrected itself flamboyantly each spring when persimmon trees wore soft yellow flowers like gracious Southern ladies in buttercup chintz. It had its Persimmon Festival in early fall when the town exploded into one magnificent simmon pudding, complete with calliopes, caramel apples and cotton candy, and with hordes of tourists to be reminded, "Never pluck a persimmon. Wait 'til it's soft and orange and falls by isself!" The prize persimmon trees in Greentree put the community on the arboreal map of America and the trees themselves on the front cover of a 1992 House Beautiful magazine. Persimmon trees abounded in the fields and open woods surrounding the town and even flourished in the Town Square itself. But, it was with the particular persimmon trees located on the Centennial School lawn that I had my own eventual grievance.

As a fledgling teacher in the Greentree Community Schools, I found that these graceful trees did much to satisfy the aesthetic yearnings of my third-grade youngsters, but they interfered in great measure with one of their fundamental functions. Because of overcrowding in Greentree schools, I was assigned to teach in a portable classroom that had carpeting and air-conditioning, but no plumbing. Therefore, it was imperative that my classroom be moved smack alongside of Centennial in order to share Centennial's restrooms. But persimmon trees, a minor grove of them, prevented this. Therefore the townspeople, the school board, and the Persimmon Planning Committee thought it best to park us a good thirty feet away to protect their 'simmons, their reputations, and community pride.

Never Pluck a Persimmon then, is the story of a satellite kind of school revolving around the ponderous primary one. It is the story of Union and secession from that Union. It is a multi-focused, unpredictable series of dilemmas that will not dissolve but which do have to do with the fact that a Prize Persimmon, to a Greentree-er, is esoteric enrichment, contemporary culture,— status! And which is all very understandable, except to a lively, lovable group of youngsters and their teacher. But we'd best begin at the beginning...

Contents

PREFACE		iii
Chapter I	THE INAUGURATION OF SESQUI	1
Chapter II	THE FIRST DAY	5
Chapter III	MR. BIRLY COMES TO OBSERVE	9
Chapter IV	ART FOR ART'S SAKE	13
Chapter V	FLUTOPHONIA	17
Chapter VI	MR. JACKSON INTERVENES	22
Chapter VII	ACTION! ACTION!	24
Chapter VIII	THE SUBSTITUTE SAYS	28
Chapter IX	MRS. JACKSON AND HER COMMITTEE	32
Chapter X	THE 'SIMMONS FALL	40
Chapter XI	A STAR IS BORN	49
Chapter XII	THE SCIENCE FAIR	56
Chapter XIII	THE CLOTHING DRIVE	64
Chapter XIV	A.G.H.A.S.T.!	69
Chapter XV	G.O.T.–GREENTREE'S ORGANIZED TEACHERS	73
Chapter XVI	THE KNIGHTS FROM NEWTON'S BEANERY	77
Chapter XVII	THE MONEY DRIVE	80
Chapter XVIII	EXTRA-CURRICULAR ACTIVITIES	92
Chapter XIX	THE PEEPING TOM	96
Chapter XX	THE FIELD TRIP	101
Chapter XXI	GETTING READY	106
Chapter XXII	THE DEDICATION	111
Chapter XXIII	THE BIRTHDAY PARTY	122
Chapter XXIV	THE BIG SNOW	127
Chapter XXV	THE WAR BETWEEN THE SCHOOLS	132
Chapter XXVI	THE SIDES ARE DRAWN	140
Chapter XXVII	THE WET SPRING	145
Chapter XXVIII	THE SCHOOL BOARD RESOLVES...	150

I.

THE INAUGURATION OF SESQUI

It was my first year of teaching and I was assigned a third grade class in the town of Greentree, Indiana—population 12,000. But the assignment had as much twist to it as any intricately-woven Chinese queue from Dynasty Days. Instead of an ordinary, high-ceilinged, many-windowed, blackboarded, conventional-type of room—within the walls of a strongly-structured, small-townish, conventional-type school—I was given a just-off-the-drawing-board, experimental, portable classroom that was placed thirty feet away from three-storied Centennial Elementary like a reluctant outhouse.

"But why—why would a brand-new teacher be given all this—this Title I, II, III or whatever, luxurious government appropriation? Why wouldn't a teacher with seniority have lapped this display of Money in Education up long before any new teacher ever got near the saucer?" I asked myself, chewing on a pencil stub the day before school was scheduled to begin.

"Was I a cynic?—to be having such thoughts?" I questioned as I took note of my lavish surroundings these first minutes after my arrival in Greentree.

How could I help thinking thus? My 'black'-boards were bluegreen. In fact, they had such a Mediterranean-look to them that I kept glancing back—at the fish! My delicious-smelling paneled walls were so new there were yet fragmentary sawdust drippings in behind-the-scenes, closed-off closets—for kids?or books? But, the star on the Christmas tree was a vibrant,resilient, acrylic-fibered, wall-to-wall, kid-to-kid, lemony-beige,spot-resistant rug!

"But...why, for me?" I asked the question again.

"Why wouldn't someone with tenure get all this? Why give it to a crass greenhorn, a blatant newcomer?" I mused.

The portable classroom, manufactured by an Indiana trailer corporation had been placed thirty feet from Greentree's stately yellow-bricked Centennial to relieve classroom crowding. And, because it had been installed in Greentree's sesquicentennial year, it had immediately been tabbed "Sesqui" by an imaginative lady on the School Board.

Greentree's School Board—I learned, was tremendously farsighted. Instead of building a new school—or even putting an addition onto the old, the gap-breeching thing for forward-looking school boards to do was to buy, or even rent, one of these classrooms and place it like a new chick beside the mother hen. And as need fluctuated throughout the community, it could thus be moved hither and thither from school to school. Portable classrooms therefore had no permanent underpinnings and consequently, I had a premonition that Sesqui and all her inhabitants would be held in a kind of permanent state of flux.

This was at the moment partially verified by the suddenness with which the door to Sesqui was thrust open, putting my place of beauty through mildly titillating tremors.

It was Mr. Birly, principal of Centennial,and of this new appendage, Sesqui. Mr. Birly, a man in his middle-fifties, gives a first impression of trying to please. Looking back I can say Mr. Birly is sincere in his aims and purposes and at the same time, he tries. But because he tries so hard and is, at the same time, so terribly busy, he is extremely nervous. You get to thinking sometimes that Mr. Birly could easily develop a tic in his neck or in one of his avant garde eyes if he but had the time.

But now Mr. Birly bared his teeth in a crotchety smile and began: "How...how are you adjusting to all...all this—this—beauty?" and he gesticulated magnanimously.

"It's a gorgeous room, Mr. Birly," I assured him. "But I can't understand why one of the older teachers wouldn't have jumped at it." There was nothing to be gained by feigning naivety, I thought.

"Well—" he paused, his lips puckering into a thought-provoking expression, "They all had their chance." He kept smiling.

"And 'they' turned it down?" I kept the conversation open.

"Miss Morrow," Mr. Birly apparently changed the subject, "I do hope you haven't weak kidneys."

"Why—no I don't, but what's that got to do with.. " I was stunned by the question.

"Good," he blinked. "The lounge is over in Centennial so we won't have to worry about that."

"The lounge?..." I was mystified.

"There are no toilet facilities in Sesqui," he leveled, wanting to be done with it. "You will have to bring your children to Centennial for...for toileting," he finished. "Centennial has a great many..."

"But Sesqui," I was trying to get the picture—"Sesqui has no plumbing—then? None at all?" the impact of it all rested uncomfortably on my eyebrows.

"No. No running water of any kind. Sesqui is not connected." Mr. Birly finished the picture.

"The buzzers and bells are not connected as yet either," he said somewhat absentmindedly.

"But the plumbing is...not connected," I repeated.

"The plumbing is non-existent," Mr. Birly stressed.

I got it.

Sesqui was all mine, every little unconnected bit of her! She was primitive isolation in the center of sanitized civilization. She was an Adam's rib fashioned into a help-mate but with no excretory system! I could understand all about city budgets and taxes and school boards. But would a Castoria-addicted third-grader comprehend?

But there was one sparkling drop of dew on the grass, however, which Mr. Birly called attention to: "You will only have twenty boys and girls," Mr. Birly informed. "Sesqui wouldn't hold any more desks," he added.

"If you need anything," he further added, "shout."

Then, seeing the dismay on my face, he showed great evidence of dentists and dentifrices: "I am here to help, you know," he said softly. And he was gone.

I looked past the aquamarine blackboards, past the regally-paneled walls, over the vibrant, lemony-beige resilient rug and through my glistening windows—over to the ponderous giant, Centennial.

Were the teachers there counting books, readying their rooms for the school year ahead? Were they musing about the kind of youngsters they would be recipient to this year?

Or, were they over in the lounge inhaling all the summer gossip and wondering about me and Sesqui? Were they enjoying all their facilities? Were they wondering just what kind of relationship 'Sesqui', the faint echo, would have with baritone, booming Centennial? Were they wondering if Sesqui would conform to Centennial policies? Were they fearing that Sesqui would lead the way—or—or follow? Were they speculating about what it would be like teaching with the latest, finest and best but without the first, most-necessary, and vital?

Were they...? I looked again.

They were. Either a contingent of teachers in the lounge or a committee from the Greentree Ladies' Aid Society at the principal's office window was scrutinizing Sesqui from Centennial's elongated windows.

The eyes of many were indeed upon us—Sesqui and me.

They were wondering, I knew.

But then, so was I.

II

THE FIRST DAY

A swashbuckler of a storm heralded in the school year. Rain and hail blustered into Greentree in such quantities and with such force that windows were cracked, limbs were torn abruptly from trees, and an unabashed fury like Judgment Day was felt across the plains. Raincoats and rubbers subsequently were dug out from the dusty innards of community closets where they had been left forgotten from the spring before.

But school would start regardless at 9:00 a.m. and Greentree's youth would be polishing for the occasion.

And, at the appointed time they came, their eager little upturned faces like funnels waiting to receive the dosage—third grade. Their faces were something to gladden any heart—but, oh, those muddy, muddy feet—for the lemony-beige rug!

"Come in, come in!" I welcomed the first arrivals, checking report card against the master list—making sure that no child who was destined for Centennial should be banished to Sesqui.

My third-graders, I eventually discovered, ranged from seven years of age to ten. They were evenly divided—boys, ten, girls, ten. They were Americans, to be sure, but their ancestors lived a by-gone day in Scandinavia, Italy, Africa, Germany, Yugoslavia, Poland, Mexico, the British Isles and Puerto Rico. Centennial and Sesqui alike opened their arms to children whose parents were influential professional people as well as indigent migratory workers. Greentree had its share of rich and poor, privileged and underprivileged, cultured and refined children as well as some genuine ruffians. To me they seemed a heterogeneous group of youngsters—rarin' to go.

"My name is Miss Morrow," I began. "Please be seated, children."

The storm at that moment lifted Sesqui from her moorings somewhat so that the seats seemed to rise themselves in greeting.

After a mild scramble I began to arrange the children alphabetically but abandoned this in some degree when I discovered a malicious cluster of James, Jesse, Jody, Jonathan, and John bunched together like rubber bananas to the rear of Sesqui. There was confusion also from the fact that the storm had not abated and many of the Mothers chose to remain for a time.

"What a beautiful rug!" one of the Mothers commented.

"And look what we've done to it!" said another.

"I moved from the country to get my kid away from the one-room schoolhouse. Now look at what we've got!"

The children responded to their bright, new surroundings. They looked everything all over as though they were contemplating a mammoth double-dip chocolate ice cream cone. They liked Sesqui. They told me so. They liked the wood-paneling, the pretty chalkboards, and the shiny desks. Most of all, though, they liked the soft, spongy, lemony-beige rug. It was fun to feel it with your hands. It was better fun, they discovered the second day of school, to take off your shoes and then your socks to feel the soft tickles on your toes—something like a mud puddle full of spider silk.

"You can even rub stuff from your nose into it, Miss Morrow," I was told the third day of school, "and it disappears!"

A magic rug indeed!

"But were first days of school this noisy?" I asked myself. "Was the novelty of the situation—or perhaps the storm—the cause of the commotion? The Mothers were making a brand-new teacher extremely nervous:

"Will Mary have any history this year?"

"What time will they be home for lunch?"

"What time will recess be this year?"

"When are the first reports due?"

"Will you have conferences with parents this year?"

"Where did you teach before?"

"Do you live in Greentree?" the Mothers asked, while the children shouted: "She took my pencil...!"

"He stole my eraser and it was new!"

"She put gum on me..."

"Look at Johnny."

"May I leave the room?"

"Where is my locker?"

"Do we get books today?"

"When do we go home?"

"I lost my milk money."

"Do we need milk money today?"

I felt as though I were standing on a bridge under which had just roared a great steam engine. The smoke from the engine was here, there and everywhere—rising up—moving ever away from me. I could never recapture it. I had no control over it. It was there and it just kept going.

So it was with the third-graders and their Mothers. They were here, there, and everywhere, and they just kept going! The boat was rocking! Something had to give...someone had to get out...

At that moment as gallant a St. George I have ever seen—in black latex armor, which made him impervious to the weather but not to the situation, burst through Sesqui's door: "Ladies! Ladies!" he cried. "You must leave. Miss Morrow must start classes!"

Mr. Birly was here to help.

"But it's raining—hard," protested one woman who had tracked in her share of Greentree's mud.

"Come, come, we're not sugar," Mr. Birly answered. "And how do you like Sesqui?" he added, in case any feelings were hurt.

"That's why we came," answered one friendly mother. "We couldn't wait until Open House."

"Yes, come, come now," Mr. Birly continued chatting in his jovial principal way until the last of the Mothers waved to their offspring and disappeared through the door. Then he nodded his good-bye.

But one mother, and with her child, had been in one of Sesqui's modern closets.

"Miss Morrow," she whispered, "where is your bathroom?"

"Over at Centennial," I replied.

The woman looked as though she had just removed her head from a mound of sand.

"There's none here—in this building?" she apparently wanted to hear it again.

"No," I replied. "Everything's over in Centennial. That's how it is. That way," I pointed, feeling that she needed direction.

"But...but Robert..." she began feebly...

She didn't finish. Robert, in a determined, concentrated sprint, had already started for Centennial.

His mother ran to join him.

The class, I discovered when I turned to them, was now left to be itself. As its first joint effort it chose to stare bewilderingly at me. There were many questions in their young eyes: "What would we do with the year that had been given to us?"

"Would we get along with each other?"

"What would we learn?"

"Would it be hard?"

"What problems would we solve?"

For, here we were, thrust upon each other—neither of us having had a choice about the other's selection. I was their teacher. They were my pupils. And we were at the mercy of each other.

I did like what I saw. My third-graders looked eager and ready. They were combed and clean and they sat waiting expectantly..now, very quietly, very seriously.

"We'll pass out our texts," I announced, smiling my approval.

They anxiously grasped the books and returned my smile.

"Sesqui has been launched," I thought to myself. She had been Christened without so much as a bubble of champagne...

But,—I was counting on the kids.

III

MR. BIRLY COMES TO OBSERVE

By the second week of school things had settled nicely. The boys and girls were finished showing off for the new teacher. They were finished staring. They were now ready to learn.

And the subjects—reading, spelling, penmanship, math, and social studies were ticked off one by one as the day's schedule was formed and maintained. "Break time" or "bathroom time" caused the only complications.

Trying to schedule a mass trip to Centennial at the proper time was extremely difficult.

If the third grade went at 10:15 we ran into three other classes. At 10:30 it was "all clear" but it was too late for Robert Jackson, the boy who had dashed so impetuously for Centennial the first day of school.

"Look here," Robert's father had informed me one lunch hour.

"My kid not only has weak kidneys—well, it gets worse than that," he concluded.

"Perhaps he should be transferred to a third grade class in Centennial," I suggested, "to be close to the lavatories."

"Naw," he shook his head. "Robbie likes you. This is important. Leave him be."

"But," he cautioned, "when he says he's got to go—you better believe it!" I promised.

That afternoon I had begun to write the penmanship assignment on the blackboard when an authoritative knock came to Sesqui's door. It was Mr. Birly.

"I am here," he beamed, "to observe the new teacher. This is one of my duties, you know," and he smiled beamingly.

"Already?" was all I could get out.

The importance of the moment was staggering. Here was a man who held my future as a teacher in his own unadulterated opinion, and I had hardly begun. It wasn't quite fair. Why, here was the man who could make or break me!

"Class," I said, feigning composure. "Mr. Birly has come for a visit. Would anyone welcome him?"

The children, confused by my apparent phoniness, stared uncomprehendingly at both me and Mr. Birly.

"Why not sit over there, Mr. Birly?" I offered, smiling. "I have teeth too," I thought wildly, wondering what in the world I would be doing in the next few minutes. We were about to have a penmanship lesson. If I had been a "pro" I would have gone right on with the planned lesson...But I thought Mr. Birly would like to see us do something—not just write something at our desks. I thought we should perform.

"All right, now, class, put your pencils and papers away," I began nervously.

"Get out your spellers. How about turning to page ten?"

"We had that page," the class commented almost in unison. "We did that page last week."

"Kids!" I thought. "Their mouths were enormous caverns. Carlsbad. Mammoth Caves!"

"I know," I said quietly, "but I thought Mr. Birly might like to see the spelling cheers we've worked out—for our words," I added.

"Oh-h-h-h," the class was interested now. They did respond to the spelling cheers.

"May I lead 'pickle'?" Mary Jane wanted to know. Pickle was the first word on page 10.

Mary Jane was my innocent-looking, hip-swishing Marilyn Monroe.

"All right," I agreed.

Mary Jane walked to the front of the room. She had an undefinable "I know what I am about" swing to her white-pleated skirt.

She stood at attention facing the class. Then her eyes widened suddenly in a wild kind of pre-knowledge and her mouth opened: "P!" Mary Jane shouted to the class and to a startlingly open-mouthed Mr. Birly, and then she did an honest-to-goodness split.

The class followed the leader: "P!" everyone hollered, rising to the occasion and knocking two chairs over in the process. Then, in one frantic simultaneous action, the class split—as best it could wherever and whenever—on the lemony-beige rug.

"I!" Mary Jane then called, leaping to her feet and throwing her arms over her head in a mad, mad, mad world kind of gesture.

The class did likewise, their voices aiming for the sun.

Mr. Birly followed with his eyes, as best he could. They rolled in their sockets—east to west—then, surprisingly, north to south in anticipation of what was next.

"C!" Mary Jane persisted, cupping her mouth with her hands for maximum volume and then wagging her finger in a "trucking-on-down-the-avenue", her hips swaying in coordination.

"C," the class followed. Where there was no room to "truck" they made room by pushing desks and chairs impatiently out of the way. Mr. Birly looked as though he was thinking of bolting.

"K!" Mary Jane shouted over the bedlam—and then touched her toes!

"K!" the class repeated, doing likewise.

"L!" Mary Jane ordered, placing her arms at akimbo.

"L!" the class followed—building up to the climax they knew was coming.

"E! "—Mary Jane screamed, leaping three feet into the air.

"E!" the class roared, reaching an unbelievable crescendo, and hurling themselves with an intenseness that is usually reserved for volcano suicides.

"PICKLE!" Mary Jane finished off, throwing herself onto the floor in a spectacular, completely-ravished kind of splendor.

"PICKLE!" the class finished, and the whole room died—right there on the floor before Mr. Birly's very eyes.

It was Mr. Birly who scrambled to his feet first. Happiness was getting out of Sesqui as soon as possible.

"Miss Morrow," he said on his way out, "there's just one thing that needs clarifying. On the board there..." and he pointed.

"Just what had you in mind...?"

I turned to the blackboard while the class brushed imaginary dirt from dresses and pants.

There in my very own handwriting was: "THIS IS A BRA!"

I was speechless.

"Why—I don't know, Mr. Birly!"

"Well," he stammered, somewhat confused also, "whatever..."

And he was gone.

I sank soggily into my highly-polished, stocking-snaggin' chair.

I thought and thought.

It was fully ten minutes after Mr. Birly's hurried exodus that I realized THIS IS A BRA was my unfinished sentence for the penmanship lesson...THIS IS A BRAVE NEW WORLD, was what I had started to write.

But the knock had come. Mr. Birly's interruption had changed all that.

I could only stare blankly out of Sesqui's windows at the petulant prize persimmons unabashedly swaying in resplendent September fullness.

IV

ART FOR ART'S SAKE

When the morning mail arrived from Centennial one particularly rusty-rose fall morning, I was informed via a heavily scrawled note from Mr. Birly, that Miss Forester, Art Supervisor for all Greentree Community Schools would be popping in any day now to see the specimen art work my third graders had produced and to also conduct a demonstration lesson.

"Wonderful!" I thought. "I'd love to see an art lesson from a 'pro'," and I mulled over which examples of our art to show. Since school had been in session but two months Miss Forester wouldn't be expecting to see a colossus of a representation but we did have a few things. We had crayoned night scenes on large sized manila paper which featured white-crayon moonlight. And we had interesting Indian designs from colored construction paper and paste. These, tucked away in a battered folder, remained unhung since the bulletin board had not yet been installed in Sesqui. I had promised the children that their work would be put up for all the world to see,—but the art supervisor had other plans.

Miss Forester came one day with a tapping on Sesqui's door that much resembled an erratic woodpecker's response to an erratic world.

"Come in," I called, and Robert Jackson, keeper of the door, moved to usher in the visitor.

"I'm Miss Forester," the dark voice said from the aluminum doorway.

"Do come in," I greeted, trying to disguise my abject fascination for the appearance of the figure silhouetted against the thin fall sunlight.

Miss Forester was a reincarnation of the museum representations I had seen of the Hindu god Shiva, the destroyer and the restorer. Her hair, long and flowing to her shoulders, had the god's symbolic twists and turns. Her sweater, casually thrown over her back, possessed dangling armsleeves that curved gently heavenward at the wrist areas, giving the impression of four arms!

"I'm Miss Morrow," I shook only one of the hands.

"I'll look at your specimen drawings at the end of the period," she informed.

"Now, class," Miss Forester announced dramatically, "we're going to have a lesson in paper sculpture. It is a lesson in abstract paper sculpture."

Although I knew abstract was a word few third-graders anywhere would comprehend, we began passing out the paper, blunted scissors, and paste with no further explanations.

Miss Forester stood at the front of Sesqui with scissors and paper poised while I crouched with the paste in the rear of the room. Then, she began: "Make a cut!" She demonstrated.

"Take a twist!" She took one.

"Dab a bit of paste! HOLD!" The "hold" was shouted in such an emphatic, do-it-or-else way the class seemed to be holding on to their chairs for dear life.

"Make a cut! Take a twist! Dab some paste! HOLD!" Shiva sing-songed. Soon the class chanted in unison: "Make a cut!"

"Take a twist!"

"Dab some paste!"

"H-O-L-D!"

Miss Forester dashed from this child to that, snipping here and dabbing there. She would look askance at an unfinished sculpture as if in great thought. Then she would sigh profoundly: "How interesting! HOW VERY, VERY INTERESTING!" Then she would dash off leaving the sculptor contemplating his or her model.

"What was it that was so very interesting?"

"What was it that Miss Forester saw that is hidden to me?" My eyes remained riveted to the paper sculptures.

After all the paste had been distributed, I took upon myself the job of passing the basket. In spite of my weak attempts, however, the lemony-beige rug soon resembled New York's Fifth Avenue after a President or an astronaut went through.

"Now," Miss Forester said delightedly, and only in a half-shout when the last dab of paste had found its mark, "let's see what we've made!"

"What have we here?" she asked Henry Burnett in the first row who was staring at his 'thing' perched in front of him like a vulture about to take flight.

"I don't know," he said. "I've got a lot of twisted and stuckup paper."

"But what does it look like?" Miss Forester persisted, looking at his sculpture as though she had just discerned the riddle of the Sphinx in its intricate folds.

"I think it looks like a mashed banana," Mary Jane volunteered.

"It don't look like nothing to me," commented Henry glumly.

"Come, now. Let's use our imaginations!" Miss Forester prompted. It was the ink-blot test all over again.

"Mine looks like my Uncle Harry on Saturday nights," said the smarty in the back row.

"Here are Mr. Birly's eyes," volunteered Sandy with the yellow braids.

"Well, study them for a moment while I ask Miss Morrow to show me your sample work," Miss Forester gave me the cue. I immediately took out the large folder and placed it on the little library table so that I could spread out the children's work with ease.

The moon scenes were the first to fall under the artist's scrutinizing gaze. One after the other of the scenes was placed onto the table while the children looked for approval and I myself waited for professional comment. None was forthcoming. Miss Forester said nothing.

When the last moon was orbited onto the table I physically turned to face her. She stood staring at the artwork. Then, licking her pale dry lips she began in a harsh whisper: "Miss Morrow. I understand this is your first year of teaching."

"Yes," I affirmed. "It is."

"Well, then," she spoke authoritatively, "you must never, never never paint or crayon the moon like this."

"What do you mean—like this?" I was dumbfounded.

"Your moons are all waning," she stated a fact.

"Yes?" I did not get the point. "How could she tell without a calendar?" I wondered.

"You never draw a moon unless it's waxing." The lady meant it.

"But...but...what is the reason for that?" I asked, stupefied.

"Bad luck," she concluded.

With one sweep she had dismissed what she held to be twenty waning moons!

"What else have you?" she changed the subject.

I bewilderingly gathered the moons together into a scraggly, sad bundle and then reached for the Indian designs. But icy, curling fingers stopped me at design #4.

"Enough!" Miss Forester spoke in one didactic explosion. "I have seen four. I'll see no more."

"Wh-h-h-h..." I stammered.

"Do you realize what you have done?" Miss Forester demanded.

I hadn't the slightest idea, but my knees were doing a tango with my heart. My half-slip had also done an about-face. The children were on the edges of their seats. They couldn't know what was going on but they knew things were not going well.

"These are hex signs," Miss Forester stated flatly. "Indian signs my foot. No Indian ever saw these. These are Pennsylvania Dutch hex signs..."

"But...but they were on an Indian cave in..." I started to explain.

Miss Forester's voice was mounting in range: "You, Miss Morrow, with your apparent ignorance have already hexed this brand new building. Ses...Ses...?"

"Sesqui," I answered weakly.

"You must burn these at once. Before it is too late. Perhaps there is still time. These have not been hung!" she directed.

"You have placed half circles upside down and all the luck has spilled out. Do you see?"

I didn't see.

I looked at the boys and girls. They looked as helpless as I felt. They looked as though they knew Sesqui had been hexed. I wearily scooped up the art work and stuffed everything back into the bulging folder.

"Goodbye, children," Miss Forester was saying to the class.

"I'll be sure to tell Mr. Birly—how things are, over here," she said to me, nodding.

"Yes," I agreed, "be sure to tell Mr. Birly." After all, if I had hexed Sesqui Mr. Birly should be the first to know.

Miss Forester disappeared into the waning sunlight. I sank slowly into my chair while the children looked to me for guidance.

What could I say?

What was the use?

Sesqui was doomed.

Shiva had spoken.

V

FLUTOPHONIA

"Miss Morrow," Mr. Birly called to me the very next sunspeckled morning. "Could you have your flutophone players ready for the pep assembly on Friday afternoon? We'd like a little music—to cheer the players up, you know."

The players needed cheering. They had lost five games out of the five played...Perhaps more than Sesqui was hexed...

"We'd be glad to," I assured Mr. Birly, honored to be asked.

It was as it should be. There were Pom-Pom girls from Centennial's fifth grade—there were baton twirlers from the fourth. It was only fitting and proper that there be flutophone players from the third.

"We'll be ready," I smiled to Mr. Birly.

While a seldom seen band director did assume the responsibility at Centennial for rarely-heard but genuine music, the individual classroom teacher was required to participate in a pre-instrument method in his or her own classroom—to see which pupils might come up with a hankering for tootling and thus provide material for the band.

So it was that twenty flutophones found their way to the third graders and to me.

The pre-instrument method was such that before a child played anything made of wood or brass, he or she played around with something plastic. The flutophone cost $1.00. A clarinet, a flute, a saxophone of course constituted major investments. Hence, for a pittance, a mother and father could know whether they housed a player-piano-roll-inserter under their roof, or, a Van Cliburn.

And there were other advantages. By following the pre-instrument plan, the child acquired an elementary knowledge of music and rhythm. This made the transfer to the real thing a smooth operation. Then, too, an ocarina, a tonette, and a flutophone—or whatever—were much easier to blow. Fussing with a reed and learning to purse lips into a prudently purposeful pucker presented problems.

"Children," I told the class that afternoon. "Mr. Birly wants us to play our flutophones at the next pep assembly. But we have much practicing to do. Let's begin with 'Here We Go 'Round the Mulberry Bush'...a deep breath, now. Ready?"

"May I have a Kleenex first?" Mary Jane held us back.

When all was settled again I turned to the piano.

"Blow!" I yelled. And we blew.

"Here We Go 'Round the Mulberry Bush" resounded through Sesqui. This was our finest song. We blew and blew and went and went. 'Round and 'round. Again and again and again.

I could visualize my twenty pupils—twenty years hence—collectively collapsed on a Master Psychiatrist's couch saying: "We'd have been all right. If only we could have played our songs on the real thing. But flutophones...

Mr. Birly wanted flutophones at the assembly. I was determined he should have them.

"Remember," I told the class. "Whatever happens—the show must go on. Once you start playing at the football assembly—no matter if you lose a tooth or your nose starts to bleed—you keep right on playing."

And when the day came—we were ready. We had tootled and tootled and tootled. And so we marched into the Valley of—to the assembly.

Looking back I see now that it is regretful that small children today are seldom exposed to the old-fashioned, three-ring, sawdusted, cotton-candied circuses in the raw which their parents enjoyed. By seeing all the animals in their wild savagery,—by smelling their animal smells—by being eye-witness to all the fantastic movements of the agile acrobats—all this gave a slice of life to the former generation that adequately prepared them for football pep assemblies!

But walking my Sesqui-oriented, TV-addicted, Miss-Morrow-sheltered youngsters to the very center of howling, teeming, screaming humanity was like putting twenty marshmallows into a 500° oven! It was deserting twenty lambs in the midst of a ravaging, terrifying, western-plains blizzard.

Not that I really deserted—but who or what matters when the bass drum is thumping

"GO-GO-GO".
and every kid in creation is yelling
"SHOW-SHOW-SHOW"
whoever-it is that they've got

"GUTS-GUTS-GUTS"
no if's or
"BUTS-BUTS-BUTS!!!"

Mr. Birly was there! He was smiling in his crotchety way!

And the Pom-Pom girls were all red and blue crepe paper fluttering in synchronized precision. And the baton twirlers were sporadic flashings of silver and gold. And there, in the midst of it all—taking it all in—in regal, reigning majesty, and tied to an eighth-grader's leather-gloved arm, sat the mascot, the CENTENNIAL EAGLE!

Expressionless, filmed eyes contemplated the mad surroundings. What was the eagle thinking...of the Pom-Poms, the batons?...the prancing boys in football regalia,—the harsh rantings of the coach...the thundering boom-boom-booms of the ever-present, ever-thumping drums?

"The Humane Society should hear of this," I thought, staring back at the eagle. "What effect could all this have on an eagle's nervous system?"

Here was a tribal ceremony at its peak! And here were the third-graders seeing nothing but the eagle! They were mesmerized by it!

"Is he tied? For sure?"

"Can he get loose?"

"Does he like pep assemblies?" they wanted to know.

How was a non-rational being reacting to all this so-called rational confusion? The only thing I could discern was an occasional quick twisting of the head and an opening and closing of the hooked beak. From all indications, the eagle had no visible response. It remained placid, perched atop the boy's protected arm. A football helmet protected his head. The boy had moved to a floor lectern now where he rested both arm and eagle while the assembly progressed.

And still the third-graders stared. They were completely fascinated with this huge bird of prey—this symbol of America and of Centennial and of course, of Sesqui.

But the signal came for the flutophone contribution to the program to begin. To wrest the children away from contemplating the eagle was difficult, but finally, two straight lines of pre-musicians with pre-instruments were ready to play a pre-musical selection.

The noise stopped. The drums were quiet. The Pom-Poms still.

And the tootling began.

"Here We Go 'Round the Mulberry Bush..."

The contrast between what had immediately preceded the tootlers and the string of straggly notes that emitted from the frightened, confused children was overwhelming. From a rousing, raving, ranting din of boom-booms and hand-claps and shrieking, swishing, swaying cheer-leaders the atmosphere changed to the twittering tootles of twenty twittering tootlers!

It was one solitary tinkle of glass, one feeble echo, after the shattering of a gigantic department store window.

It was a blade of grass in a jungle.

It was a drop of rain after a storm.

Whatever it was—it was too much for the Centennial eagle!

While we were yet going 'round the mulberry bush—the third time, the eagle turned suddenly to its captor, and with several sharp thrusts, began jabbing its beak at the eighth-grader's helmet. The boy screamed and pushed his arm out as far as he could while the bird, completely befuddled, began flapping its huge black wings helplessly but yet ominously.

"Cut him loose!" screamed the boy.

Mr. Herendeen, the Coach, ran out onto the gym floor with penknife ready. The eighth-grader bravely held on while the black madness was cut away.

The Centennial eagle seized his opportunity then, and zoomed straight ahead and out through the gymnasium's open doors to freedom. The audience shrieked—some in approval, others in frantic dismay, while still others headed in the direction of the school nurse.

But the tootlers remained undaunted. They hadn't missed a note. Their eyes had seen the gore—and the glory—but their mouths kept at it. It mattered not that a single soul listened to their efforts. They were told the show must go on. And it did. They tootled ever onward and they sent the eagle to higher and higher other worlds, quieter worlds.

There were neighbors of Centennial who reported that before the eagle put wing to its final farewell flight it had taken immediate refuge on Sesqui. And there were children who crowded to the door of the gymnasium to wave an adieu who said that it swooped in salute once over Centennial and then over Sesqui and then it was off!

Whatever the story, Mr. Birly took matters into his own hands by rushing out onto the gymnasium floor and announcing over the microphone that Centennial's mascot had belonged to the Greentree Zoo and that Centennial would no doubt be billed for its loss.

Never Pluck a Persimmon

"I'll give a reward for its safe return," he shouted to the now disemboweled assembly.

With a nod I disbanded the tootlers. "We're looking for a bird!" became the slogan of the day.

"What'd he do?" suspicious townspeople's eyebrows went up when a teacher posed the question.

But the eagle was gone. It had disappeared into the heavens like a child's helium-filled balloon going up, up, up to infinity.

Without the good-luck mascot to rely on, Centennial lost another game, 67–0. Sesqui had apparently jinxed things again.

Mr. Birly never again asked the flutophone players to furnish music for a special occasion. But it didn't matter. In just two more weeks the third-graders had tootled their last. They had graduated to the real thing. The Band Director had seen fit to issue them genuine instruments. They could now drink milk from a glass.

VI

MR. JACKSON INTERVENES

But one day, about two weeks after "Grandma's Old-Fashioned Soap" won a blue ribbon in the Science Fair and complimentary cakes subsequently ate through the aluminum soap-holders in the Ladies Room in Centennial—Robert Jackson's luck ran out. He was consequently sent home at 9:55 a.m. I had gone through the proper channels to dismiss him and I considered the incident closed. But Mr. Jackson chose otherwise.

It was during my lunch hour that I was summoned to Mr. Birly's office—via a hastily-written note!

"Mr. Jackson is coming to see me at 1:00 concerning your sending his son Robert home this a.m. I would like you to be present also at this meeting to answer any questions that might come up. I will send someone to take over your class at 12:55 that you may be here on time."

Of course it was signed by Mr. Birly.

"So be it," I thought, wondering about the outcome of such an encounter.

When I walked into the severely-paneled, primly-polished office, I found Mr. Birly in the final stages of consuming his lunch. A large red thermos of coffee with a matching red cup, alongside, was in evidence in addition to a half of liverwurst sandwich and some vaguely-shimmering orange jello in a colorless, opaque plastic container.

"I have been on that phone constantly," Mr. Birly chomped.

"Haven't had time to eat. Please be seated, Miss Morrow," and he gulped politely.

I sat, but no sooner had the chair met the back of my lap than I heard a rough, coarse voice demanding: "Where is 'e?"

Mr. Birly was nonplussed.

"Sit down, Miss Morrow," he further chomped. "My secretary will take care of whoever it is."

But she didn't—or couldn't.

What happened next is seared in a memory that has traced and retraced every little wild detail.

It was a raving Mr. Jackson who suddenly thumped into the innards of Mr. Birly's private office.

Never Pluck a Persimmon

Sensing some kind of a showdown, Mr. Birly shoved the last bite of sandwich into his mouth and was halfway to a standing position when he was solidified into absolute immobility.

"I brung ya somethin'," Mr. Jackson snarled between clenched teeth as he tore open a small brown paper bag. Then, with one violent sweep of a gesture he scooped up and then slammed down one very-much-messed, stained pair of underpants,—onto Mr. Birly's highly-glossed, clearly blottered, highly styled desk!

"Now," said a semi-satisfied Mr. Jackson in a semi-satisfied tone, "what are ya goin' ta do about it?"

Mr. Birly's secretary had followed Mr. Jackson into the room—a reincarnated mummy hanging on to the edge of blustering, volatile humanity. She—like Mr. Birly and myself—stared incomprehensibly at the condition of the desk.

The thermos had been knocked over. The jello trembled slightly now—a fact due to the strange addition of what appeared to be a miscolored cherry at its crest! The snowy blotter, which had until now opened its pores only to ink, soaked in an incongruous concoction of coffee and urine!

It was as though an uncouth, barbarian Trojan Horse had spewed its vile contents on an impeccable Mr. Birly who at the moment looked like the Abominable Snowman Abominated!

"These," Mr. Jackson found it necessary to explain, "are my kid's pants. Now you tell me—when does Sesqui get a toilet? Or do I hafta keep comin' in here—day after day—week after week? With pants like these!" he added for emphasis.

Mr. Birly's lip quivered a bit but by now he stood erect.

"You—you," he pointed straight at Mr. Jackson. "You take this—this—these pooped pants and clear out of my office before...before I call the police."

Then Mr. Birly squared his shoulders, did an about-face, and marched right out of his office leaving the cause of the debacle—the soiled pants, the quivering jello, his secretary, myself and Mr. Jackson leering unbelievably at one another.

Virginia Morrow Black

VII

ACTION! ACTION!

After school that same day when I went to see Mr. Birly about my monthly art supply requisition, I beheld a quiet, solemn, thinking man. By this time the evidence of jello and coffee and everything else had been wiped away. But what could ever wipe such a traumatic experience from Mr. Birly's fevered brain?

"Miss Morrow," he said suddenly, looking up, "do—do you, do you feel that Sesqui should have its own toilet facilities?" He had no smile to offer today.

"Well," I cautiously began. "It would be nice,—but will the schoolboard allocate the money?"

I don't think so," Mr. Birly answered sullenly. Then he asked: "Is Robert Jackson the only one who has troubles?"

"No, not really," I answered truthfully. "There are others, and, sometimes, "I put in, trepidatiously", "it is very inconvenient for the children to get on all those boots and jackets before they go to Centennial."

"Sometimes it's just too late," I added, as Mr. Birly well knew. "Couldn't Sesqui be moved nearer to Centennial?"

"Are you telling me, Miss Morrow," Mr. Birly was incredulous, "that you have no idea why your little Sesqui is parked so far away from Centennial? That you have never heard about Greentree's prize persimmon trees that are directly outside your window? Persimmon trees are more important to Greentree citizens than kids! Children do not win blue ribbons! Persimmons do!" Mr. Birly concluded, shouting.

"Well, certainly,". I defended myself. "I know that there are prize persimmon trees outside Sesqui's windows. But I did not know that they were that important."

"Important!!!" Mr. Birly continued emotionally, "The persimmon tree is to Greentree what the pine is to Christmas all over the world!"

In a more subdued tone he continued: "Greentree has persimmon festivals, persimmon cooking contests, persimmon art fairs! The whole town revolves around that so-called 'food for the gods' fruit," he added.

When Mr. Birly stopped to breathe I said: "I'll try to remember that," but the words fell on Mr. Birly's back now as he walked to the window at the rear of his office to get a fresh look at the persimmon trees. Gazing out at 'the enemy' he continued: "Long before you came, Miss Morrow, I had it out with the Board. I told them that if a satellite school—a portable classroom—was necessary, that it had to have its own facilities or else be placed smack next to Centennial."

"And you lost?" I interjected, sympathetically.

"I lost," he said flatly. "The kids lost. The trees won." Mustering more emotion he further explained: "The Board succeeded in getting the newspaper into the act. By the time everybody with a vested interest in persimmons considered Greentree without its only excitement,—well, well...persimmons were more popular than ever. New pamphlets were printed warning 'never pluck a persimmon' before it's ripe 'cause the tannin in it will pucker your mouth. Well, Greentree's been puckered up ever since about the whole mess of it, especially parents whose kids have...well, problems.

"Do you suppose," continued Mr. Birly, "That we could bring it up at the next P.T.A. meeting?"

"We?" I questioned, cautiously.

"Or a parent group—to approach the School Board with it, "he kept at it.

"Well-l..."I answered.

"Do you suppose Robert Jackson can wait 'til next meeting?" a cautious Mr. Birly asked, his eyebrows deeply furrowed.

"Why not call Mr. Jackson—or better yet, Mrs. Jackson—since she's more—ah—'reserved' than her husband, to see if she will head such a group to approach the School Board..."I suggested, little by little.

"Y-e-e-e-s-s-s," Mr. Birly was coming to the realization slowly.

"At least," I continued, "you know that the Jacksons are interested and that's half the battle."

"Y-e-e-e-s-s," Mr. Birly said. "They are interested."

"But," he added, I'll wait a day. No sense rushing things. Give them time to—ah—wash up—and all."

"Yes," I concluded, gathering up my art supplies and gaining courage for the future.

Why, Mr. Birly feared crackpots like Mr. Jackson just as much as I feared Mr. Birly, I had discovered. Mr. Birly was a pretty good Joe after all. He was even human.

I put the art supplies on the shelves in the closet over in Sesqui. My, but my beautiful room was hot! The place was burning up! But the thermostat said only 73 degrees! I put my hand to my cheek. I was the thing that was burning up! Could I be coming down with something? Perhaps the air, fresh air, would help. It had been a long, hard day.

Walking the three blocks to my room in Mrs. Decklebaum's cheerful little house, I had time to think. I was glad to have a quiet place. Mrs. Decklebaum made little noise. She was friendly and just a trifle nosey. But then she did oppose cutting down any of the persimmon trees, too. "Something will be worked out, dearie," she'd say, over and over again. "The School Board will think of something by then." And I was waiting. But there were others—like little Robert Jackson, who had waited about as long as he could...And Mr. Jackson..."

My! I did not feel well. But Mr. Birly was counting on me. And my twenty pupils needed me. A nap—and all would be well.

But hours later instead of feeling revitalized it was apparent that I should never attempt Sesqui—unconnected. my. head was in a vortex! I had better call Mr. Birly so that a substitute could be notified. I looked at the clock. It was ten minutes past seven. Why, I had slept through the dinner hour! It was always best to call the evening beforehand—whenever possible, so I feverishly dialed Mr. Birly's number. "Yes?" he said into the phone after a lengthy ringing. I explained about not feeling well.

"But my lesson plans are on the desk, Mr. Birly," I assured him.

"Miss Morrow," he began in a dead-head way. "Did you just get in?"

"Why...whatever do you mean?" I stammered into the phone.

"Miss Morrow," he said again—just as flatly. "It is twenty-five minutes to three a.m."

"It's not ten minutes past seven?" I asked incredulously, looking again at my clock.

"No," Mr. Birly said disgustedly, "Can't you tell the small hand from the large one?" he asked sarcastically.

Before I could answer Mr. Birly continued: "Miss Morrow, think nothing of it. I have had the...the...misfortune of having teachers...make this...mistake oh, for various reasons...before."

"What was he thinking?" I asked myself,. my mind racing.

"And," he added benevolently, "if it will brighten up your day—or night, whichever—I did call Mrs. Jackson and she agreed to head the committee. And she also suggested that Mr. Jackson be appointed to lead it in some way—a Privy Counselor, of sorts, I suppose."

"A Privy Counselor," I repeated.

":Yes. Privy counselor,of sorts," Mr. Bily added. "And now," he continued, "good-night…or good-morning…whichever, Miss Morrow. I will call a substitute at an appropriate hour, of course."

"Of course," I agreed weakly.

"Do get well," he finished off.

"Y-e-e-s-s-s-s," I thanked him weakly, placing the phone in its cradle. I wondered: "Did he mean it?"

But Mr. Birly was a good principal. He had a right to his thoughts I supposed. But what must he be thinking now of the third grade teacher who occupied the thorn in his side—Sesqui?

Perhaps this substitute would be the answer. She would show the world that she could handle Mr. Birly, the Sesqui-ites, and Sesqui itself—connected or unconnected. Perhaps she would even do such a tremendous job that Mr. Birly would ask her to stay. Perhaps my place was about to be usurped!

But how could I care? A monster hot pepper held me prisoner in fiery claw-like appendages. To struggle would be thowing one grain of sand against a gargantuan steel wall. I was a popsicle-stick of a sailboat competing in the America's Cup.

Perhaps the substitute could succeed where I failed. Perhaps she would even end up getting Sesqui connected. Well, I wished her luck and just in time. I was swallowed up by a Leviathan caterpillar whose insides were as warm, dark and soft as a hot chocolate éclair's on a Saturday night.

VIII

THE SUBSTITUTE SAYS

It was not until I returned to school the following week that I ascertained to what an extent Mrs. Puternaugh, the substitute, took over.

For some reason regular teachers, especially regular <u>new</u> teachers, fear substitutes, and well they should. The substitute often has been around and knows the angles. The substitute has, for instance, the advantage of looking into the teacher's messy closet, of rooting around in the teacher's own private drawers, and of finally complaining to the Principal about the lousy lesson plans. It is the substitute who has the vantage point. She is in the position to criticize—something like the Opposition Party.

On the other hand the substitute, like a replacement on a football team, feels herself that she is considered somewhat of a second-class citizen by some of the narrow-minded regular teachers and so sets out to prove that this is not the case.

Mrs. Puternaugh, unfortunately, was one who set out to prove that this certainly was not the case.

Mrs. Puternaugh, therefore, spent Monday in sizing up Sesqui. By Tuesday morning when she learned that her services would be needed the entire week, she realized that she would have the time to get things squared away and prove her salt. It was therefore Tuesday afternoon that she directed the shampooing of Sesqui's lemony-beige rug.

"Everybody took a turn with the amplifier," Clifford complained.

"Applicator," Mary Jane corrected.

It was really a sweeper," put in Justin.

"Didn't you do any lessons?" I inquired, wondering how the playing-janitor bit was going over with their parents.

"Sure," said Clifford. "We got lots of work done. You didn't get a chance at the amplifier if you didn't have your work done first."

In addition to the lovely clean rug I noted that the bulletin board which had been reclining in my closet since September was now hung.

"Wonderful!" I thought to myself, reaching into my desk for the Plan Book. But it wasn't in its usual place. My desk had been so completely cleaned it looked empty!

Never Pluck a Persimmon

I then took a tissue and blew my nose. The ravages of the fever and cold had left me with a semi-runny nose. And, reaching to deposit the tissue in the paper basket I discovered a neatly foil-lined basket now.

"Miss Morrow," Sandy raised her hand. "How are we going to salute the flag this morning?"

"The way we always do," I answered.

"But, which country is that?" Sandy persisted, pointing over my head.

I looked up.

What I saw could have been Monet's "Impression of America" but it was not the American flag. "Wh...wh...wh..." I started to ask.

"Mrs. Puternaugh washed it!" Mary Jane explained.

"With a strong detergent," Clifford confided.

"Perhaps the semaphore people could make something out of that," I thought glumly to myself, "but now I must requisition a new flag from Mr. Birly."

It was time to begin the day. I walked to the piano to play the opening bars of "The Star-Spangled Banner" which the third-graders were just beginning to learn. The peculiar sounds which emitted from that keyboard startled the entire room. Here was a tinny turn-of-the-century harpsichord—a calliope with its stuffing knocked out.

"Miss Morrow," explained Sandy. "Mrs. Puternaugh washed the insides of the piano out on Friday."

That was that. By the time the soundboard dried out...

I looked around for more 'improvements'...

The closet door had a new coat of varnish on it. There were four more coat hangers added to the one that had already been there. The chalk ledge had been waxed.

"How do you like the pencil-sharpener fixings?" asked Mary Jane, the tone of her voice indicating that her eyebrows were raised.

It was hard to believe. Installed over the pencil sharpener itself—on the side of the wall—at a height the children could reach was an overhanging, ornate bed-lamp.

"Mrs. Puternaugh said we could have it," Clifford found it necessary to explain. "She said we could see when we had a sharp point—better."

My sharp points were mentally digging into Mrs. Puternaugh when a knock came to the door. Mr. Birly burst into the room as though he had been abruptly shot out of a cannon.

"Miss Morrow. Am I glad to see you back. I refuse to order toothbrushes for everyone ln this class..."

"Toothbrushes?" I did not understand.

"Toothbrushes!" Mr. Birly answered. "Here is the requisition that that Mrs. Puternaugh put through to me. Now I feel this way. I believe in dental hygiene as much as any Principal. But when it's complicated enough...getting over to Centennial just to...just to..."

"I understand," I answered.

"Well, I came over to try to talk you out of toothbrushes. I thought perhaps maybe Mrs. Puternaugh tried to persuade you by phoning you while you were sick..."

"No, Mr. Birly," I assured him.

"And, Miss Morrow," he continued, "while we're on the subject I wanted to ask if I can turn the water off now—now that she's gone," he added.

"The water? What water?" I was baffled.

"The custodian says the constant trickle is creating rivulets in the lawn." Mr. Birly pointed out Sesqui's window to a nearby young persimmon tree whose lower branches were supporting the nozzle of a green garden hose—Sesqui's running water!

But I could see what he was talking about. The constant trickle was causing groovings in the Centennial lawn and...what could be worse than that except maybe a flooded petunia bed?

"May I leave the room for a drink of water?" the voice said from behind Mr. Birly and me. It was Unita with a plastic cup in tow.

"You see," Mr. Birly now turned to Unita. "I did buy those cups for Mrs. Puternaugh but I refuse to buy toothbrushes for after their lunch!"

"You bought twenty cups?" I asked Mr. Birly. "But where are they?"

"They're in our desks—with our names painted on them—so the germs..." Clifford began. "My Dad painted on all our names," Justin interrupted. "Mrs. Puternaugh called him up."

"You see. You see," Mr. Birly put in. "That woman wants to take over...I'm going out there and turn that hose off. It's wasting Centennial's water. Come with me over to Centennial, little girl," Mr. Birly addressed Unita, "and be sure to leave that...that cup here."

"We'll use our cups when we water-color," I told the class after Mr. Birly and Unita had gone.

So Mrs. Puternaugh's sanitation sallies had upset Mr. Birly!

I continued to secretly resent and silently ridicule Mrs. Puternaugh's unwarranted and unwanted interference until precisely at 1:30 that afternoon. For it was at this very moment that a tap-tap-tapping and a rap-rap-rapping was heard at one of Sesqui's windows—the one nearest Centennial.

"Miss Morrow," Sandy said, looking up from her work, "there's a message for you from Mr. Birly." She pointed to the window.

"I couldn't imagine..."

But when I got to the window there was but one thing for me to do! Open it and remove the message that was attached to a pulley with a single giant paper clip!

What an ingenious device!

The rope ran straight over to Centennial—to Mr. Birly's very office window.

"Dear Miss Morrow," the message read. "Mrs. Jackson called and said that her P.T.A. Committee will be having a short meeting in the lounge over in Centennial immediately following dismissal today. They would like you to be present if at all possible." Signed, Mr. Birly.

Such an intriguing time-saver!

Such an ingenious foot-saver!

Such a...Mrs. Puternaugh was a whirlwind!

"SO!" I concluded, in a matter of seconds. "In spite of the fact that Mrs. Puternaugh's short stay could be generally described as disruptive, disturbing and disastrous, I, from that instant on, had a new slant on the woman. When other teachers complained of her means I would defend her ends. When others dubbed her "nebnose" or "nosey', I would label her as "genuinely interested'. If anyone called her "neurotic" I would reclassify it as "highly imaginative" for, from where I could see it, Mrs. Puternaugh had accomplished the nigh-impossible.

In one short week she had succeeded in getting Sesqui connected already!

IX

MRS. JACKSON AND HER COMMITTEE

"Now," I said to my at-the-moment wriggling, disinterested class, "we're going to have a lesson on how to give speeches before a group. There is a P.T.A. Committee that has asked that a few of you participate in a skit they are preparing. Although I understand you may only have a few lines to say—or perhaps only act out something—pantomime it—I do want you to know how to stand up before an audience. Now," I continued, "I think we will start with a 'show and tell' speech. You did this in Kindergarten and in the first and second grades. I'm sure you can do it again."

"A 'show and tell' speech is the easiest kind of speech," I enthused. "You bring in a toy or a game—or anything you find interesting and tell the class about it. Talk about it. Demonstrate it. Tell us how it works."

"What about a pet?" Sandy wanted to know. "Can we tell how it works?"

"No pets," I was firm.

"Nothing that moves."

"What about a battery-operated truck? It moves," Robert asked.

"How about a seahorse?" scientist Justin Mackin wanted to know.

"Only dead ones," I replied. "Now you are to stand nice and tall...don't lean on the desk—hands at your sides—or, holding your object. You must speak loudly enough so that everyone can hear you..."

"Are there any questions?" I came up for air.

"I'd like to bring in my Mother's gallstones from her operation," said Clifford sadly, "but they're lost."

"Yes. We were all through that," I replied. "Whatever interests you," I further explained. "Talk it over with your parents. We'll have our speeches on Friday. Robert's Mother, Mrs. Jackson, is coming to listen and to pick out those of you she wants for the P.T.A. skit." And the instructions were complete.

By the time Friday arrived I had a pretty good idea of the subjects to be demonstrated, but of course it was all new to Mrs. Jackson who sat on the edge of her seat as though she was about to sip the nectar of the gods.

Justin Mackin led the list.

"This here rock at one time was in a dinosaur's stomach," declared Justin, displaying a smooth-surfaced rock the size of a large potato.

"How do you know?" Mrs. Jackson raised her hand.

"Because," he answered authoritatively, "It has smoothness. It was worn smooth by dinosaur juices over a period of time." Justin read the Book of Knowledge like it was a Big-Little book.

"But where did you find this—this interesting stone?" asked Mrs. Jackson as though she were inquiring about the Rosetta Stone.

"In my own back yard. On top of the trash heap," Justin further explained.

Mrs. Jackson was crestfallen! She did come to life somewhat, however, when Mary Jane demonstrated how she could spin a top in the center of her stomach while lying flat on the floor.

Sandy's subject was cocoons, and she allowed each child to shake her collection: "Hear the moth or butterfly inside?" she would ask with her big blue eyes that had a sense of wonder to them. When each child had shaken and heard she placed her cocoons on the science table for a permanent resting place beside the elephant's tusk, the framed ant colony, the dried manure, and the fish skeletons that were already there.

It was Henry Burnett, however, whose subject created the most interest. His topic was "My Operation". He told Mrs. Jackson, the class, and myself about his stay in the hospital—the wearing of hospital gowns, and all about the buzzer that you pushed for a nurse to appear. When he discussed how the doctors are paged, however, and how he managed to swallow (horse pills), I admit my mind wandered. But, fortunately for posterity, both Mrs. Jackson and I awoke at the appropriate moment: "And here," Henry was saying majestically as he zipped down his pants, "is the scar from my hernia operation."

Even though Mrs. Jackson was to the rear of Sesqui and I was near the cedar-lined coat closet—we got there in time. Together we held up his pants while I nonchalantly told the class about the incisions which we do, of necessity, keep to ourselves. Mrs. Jackson re-zipped the pants as though she could have done it blindfolded. I had a suspicion that Henry might be charging admission for a peek in the future, but for now at least the children, Mrs. Jackson, and myself had been spared.

Eventually, the selections for the skit were made and Mrs. Jackson sent a note informing me which children would be needed. There were parts for A Statue, A Snowman, A Toy Soldier, A Carrot, A Chimney, A

Telephone Pole, A Church, A Scarecrow, A Pilgrim, A Painting, A Testube, and A Rocket. It was such an incongruous gathering of characters that I could hardly imagine the play.

But I should have known that Mrs. Jackson and her committee would come up with something really different.

It was an unsuspecting group of teachers, parents, and School Board Members who convened that stark January night—for education—for the children of the community—for doughnuts and coffee. The minutes of the previous meeting were read, the business of the day discussed, and it was time for the skit to begin.

I had been told that a choral group composed of the P.T.A. Ladies would carry the thread of the story with my boys and girls filling in slightly. I had no idea that this same thread would develop into a monstrous, thick bull rope under the inflections of the lovely "Light Voices" and the sombre "Dark Voices."

The lights dimmed. Twelve P.T.A. women marched onto Centennial's brilliantly-lighted stage followed by A Statue, A Snowman, A Toy Soldier, A Carrot, A Chimney, A Telephone Pole, A Church, A Scarecrow, A Pilgrim, A Painting, A Testube, and A Rocket. And, before a gaping Greentree audience, the tale of MICHAEL ZIG-ZAGGLE unfolded:

	"Michael's a boy who can't sit still," the Light Voices began.
	"He's full of wiggles and waggles. That is why the school work he does,—Is full of ziggles and zaggles!"
HEAVY VOICES:	"But why can't Michael concentrate—and sit still—at his little desk?"
HEAVIER STILL VOICES:	"Is it because he sits over in Sesqui?"
LIGHT VOICES:	"His Teacher tries..."
CHORUS:	"Oh—how she tries...
	"Michael," she said, "while you are doing your work let's pretend you're a statue, straight and tall. You stand in a palace, in a great hall. Now you can't move a muscle—nothing at all. You're still...very still...
	"(And the statue <u>WAS</u> still)...

Never Pluck a Persimmon

HEAVY VOICES:	until "First a little wiggle, then a big waggle, and all of Michael's work was a BIG ZIG-ZAGGLE! And the Teacher said: "Michael! You moved! You're not pretending! Now listen...and do as I say."
CLIFFORD THE STATUE:	"But Teacher, I stood, stiff and straight as I could—But Centennial is so far away!"
CHORUS:	"The knowledge of knowing 'there is none' is too much for little Michael. But, the Teacher tried again."
LIGHT VOICES:	"Michael," she said, "while Teacher is teaching today let's pretend you're a snowman, stiff with the cold. You can't move; you must stay the way that you're rolled. you're still…..very…..still (And the snowman WAS still) ...until
HEAVY VOICES:	"First a little wiggle, then a big waggle, And all of Michael's work was a BIG-ZIG-ZAGGLE! "And the Teacher said: "MICHAEL! You're wriggling! Just look at your work! Now tell me—why can't you do better?"
SANDY THE SNOWMAN:	"Teacher, I'm sorry, but I got so cold, And the colder I got, well—the wetter!"
CHORUS:	"The knowledge of knowing 'there is none' is too much for little Michael. But—the Teacher tried again..."
LIGHT VOICES:	"Michael," she said, "while Teacher is teaching today let's pretend you're a toy soldier in a tall hat. You march to the strains of rat-a-tat-tat. With a gun on your shoulder, you couldn't look bolder. So, sit nice and still...very still...

	"(And the toy soldier <u>WAS</u> still...) ...until
HEAVY VOICES:	WIGGLE...WAGGLE.. ZIG-ZAGGLE! The Teacher dipped her pen slowly in the ink "Michael," she said, "just what am I to think?"
ROBERT JACKSON	"Well, Teacher, I'm sorry that I cause you such trouble. May I leave now for Centennial?
THE TOY SOLDIER CHORUS:	And on the double?" "The knowledge of knowing 'there is none' is too much for little Michael. But—the Teacher tried again..."

(As soon as the toy soldier had finished his piece the <u>telephone pole</u> told how it had been riddled by a wood-pecker—and on the way to Centennial and the bathroom—and the <u>church</u> explained that it had bats in its belfry and therefore couldn't sit still—(and everyone who opposed "connecting Sesqui" also had bats in their belfries)—but it was the painting that really had a message—)

LIGHT VOICES:	And Teacher tried again.. "Michael," she said, "while Teacher is teaching today let's pretend you're a painting of a famous American...Let's say George Washington, gallant and tall. Now pictures don't move; they stay on the wall. So remember you're still...very still..." (And the painting <u>WAS</u> still)... until
HEAVY VOICES:	Wiggle...Waggle...ZIG-ZAGGLE! "There you are Michael! You did it again! I can't understand what you are thinking!"
CARL THE PAINTING:	"But Teacher," said Michael, "I know I am famous but that doesn't stop me from st—..."

Never Pluck a Persimmon

HEAVY VOICES:	"Studying!" The knowledge of knowing 'there is none' was too much for Michael Zig-Zaggle. But the Teacher tried again.
LIGHT VOICES:	"Michael," she said, "while Teacher is teaching today let's pretend you're a test-tube, you're all made of glass. You're standard equipment for a chemistry class. You're stiff and you're straight. You're scientifically great. But test-tubes can't move. So be very still. (And the test-tube WAS still) ...until
HEAVY VOICES:	WIGGLE...WAGGLE...ZIG-ZAGGLE! "Michael! Get over here—and get off the floor!"
HENRY BURNETT THE TEST-TUBE:	"But Teacher, that test-tube was loaded! Little pieces of glass flew all through the air...I'm sorry, but I just EXPLODED!"
HEAVY VOICES:	And all because of the knowledge of knowing "there is none."
LIGHT VOICES:	"We'll try it once more, Michael," said the Teacher. "All right," she said, "while Teacher is teaching today, let's pretend you're at Cape Kennedy. You're a stiff, straight rocket, pointed up to the sky. Someday real soon, you'll be ready to fly. But for now you're still. Very still. (And the rocket WAS still) ...until
HEAVY VOICES:	WIGGLE...WAGGLE...ZIG-ZAGGLE! "Michael! You ziggled! I'm tired of your nonsense!"
RANDY THE ROCKET:	"But Teacher, you did say that soon, the rocket would fly straight up through the sky, and it DID, 'cause I'm now ON THE MOON!"

HEAVY VOICES:	"...WHERE THERE COULD BE FACILITIES!"
LIGHT VOICES:	"Then, slowly, Michael's Teacher put down her book. "Go—Michael Zig-Zaggle!" she said.
	Then Michael's Teacher shook her head slowly, smiled to herself, and said:
EVERYONE:	"My Michael's a boy who tries to sit still but often he wiggles and waggles. I do declare—if we show him we care—We'll remove all the ziggles and zaggles!"

...And with this the entire personage swept into an all-encompassing bow. The applause came then, hesitant, sporadic, a sprinkle here, a sharp thunderclap there. It was a stupefied, half-hearted, confused kind of response. Never before had anyone present been exposed to the likes of MICHAEL ZIG-ZAGGLE in any of his or her dealings. Was it any wonder that the reaction was one of bewilderment?

It was Mrs. Jackson now who stepped out of line to say: "So let's get Sesqui connected. The knowledge of knowing there is none is too much for Michael Zig-Zaggle. Let's help him sit still over in Sesqui," she continued shouting like a cheerleader about to be replaced, "by getting behind this P.T.A. Committee!"

Now the P.T.A. President strode to the platform: "We have coffee, cookies and warm doughnuts now—to the back of the hall," she announced.

The relieved audience rose now from the seats and walked slowly to the rear of the auditorium. The semi-numbed School Board was the last to avail itself of the refreshments. Mr. Webster, I noted, wore a haunted look. John Calhoun Jones shifted his weight from the right to the left foot and then back again as though he was not quite sure where he wanted it, and Mr. Clay looked as though he had a grenade in his pocket with the pin pulled.

As Sesqui's teacher, I tried to avoid making comments on the play. After all, what could I say? Those were my kids up there...and even though I could swear to it that there had never been a ziggle nor a zaggle in any of their work because of Sesqui's distance from Centennial's restrooms—well, I did want Sesqui connected as much as any of them.

By this time I took note of the refreshment table's centerpiece which was mildly interesting. Delicately-tinted paper carnations made up the flower arrangement. They were pink and white and... "But you would think they could have used real flowers," I started to think.

"Very pretty," a woman to my left put in, "for toilet tissue."

"Surely..." I thought, but I needn't have.

I had already seen the doughnuts that were being served. They were the widest-holed, thinnest...but it was not their shape. It was rather where each rested. Each doughnut was perched around the rim of every coffee cup! Then, on top of the doughnut lay a flat round cookie. The doughnut and the cookie were fastened to the cup's handle by an ingenious small ribbon. Here was a reasonable facsimile of a commode!—The bowl,—the cup; the doughnut,—the seat; and the lid,—the cookie! HOLY JEHOSHAPHAT! Was this for real!?

"Coffee?" the woman with the frumpy burgundy hat asked, poking the silver pot questioningly at me.

I nodded, dumfounded, taking one of the 'arrangements.'

"Open your lid!" she demanded.

I swung back the cookie component which now left only the doughnut 'seat' still perched onto the rim of the cup.

The coffee was poured through the gaping hole.

"Sugar and cream?" the lady with the hat asked.

"No, thank you," I mumbled, for who needs sugar and cream when they are bearing in their own unadulterated hands—the secret of the universe? Was this—this arrangement—the magic lamp from which the genie—a connected Sesqui—was supposed to emerge? Was this blatant display of creativity-without-taste the harbinger of perhaps more primitive days to come? I thrust a dainty silver spoon through the 'hole' and stirred furiously.

Somehow I knew that such determination and unabsorbed creativity would succeed in getting Sesqui connected but good—someday, in the very near future.

X

THE 'SIMMONS FALL

It came so gradually—as Mrs. Decklebaum had promised. It came so suddenly, as Mrs. Decklebaum had cautioned. The 'simmons fell and the four day Fall Festival was upon us. Over now were all the puckerings and tastings, the plannings and the executions of all those plans. Anticipation had climbed to the very rims of all the pudding pans in Greentree and was now about to spill over and out into its very heart. At last! Greentree's gigantic 'simmon pudding was about to be popped into the oven and savored!

Every available charcoal oven had been readied for the spectacular avalanche of Indiana's choicest, yellow-cobbed corn. The butter pots were polished to a fine glitter and the new sterile butter brushes, purchased through the Persimmon Planning Committee's wholesale catalogue, were ready to be put to use. The womenfolk took out their sheer frilly aprons from the finegrained bottoms of aromatic cedar chests and some of the older women, preferring those of feed-sack texture, subjected these to a heavy-duty starching in order that they could withstand the vicissitudes of the festival. A heaving, rollicking calliope had been rented from a Miami, Florida circus company, and five thousand fryers had been ordered from nearby farms for the lavish Town Square barbecue. The highlight of the entire Festival, however, was the Persimmon Pudding Contest sponsored by the local Jaycees, in reality, the Jayshees. All the women of Greentree—of cooking age—would be vieing with one another for the honor of turning out the prize pudding of the year.

Mrs. Decklebaum, I understood, had entered the pudding contest each year, and each year won an honorable mention ribbon. "Always a bridesmaid, never a bride," she lamented, stirring her pudding mixture furiously with a large wooden spoon. "But I wouldn't consider passing a persimmon pudding contest by. It gets in your blood," she continued. "Like rentin' out to tourists who come at festival time. I wouldn't miss rentin' out. I've met some lovely people. I've had some lovely people."

"Had a banker once," she continued, slowly melding the flour now into the rich brown pulp, "from Toledo—. Then," she breathed heavily with the effort of pushing the large wooden spoon through the 'simmon mixture, "a fortune teller came another year. She was fun—from Chicago. Why," and she looked up, bragging, "I even had an undertaker and his wife, from New York. It was an off-week, so he took the time to come to a 'genuine festival' he said ours was."

Mrs. Decklebaum, being a gregarious sort of person, would enjoy something like this, I thought, amused. I could see her tourists, past and future, tiptoeing through her anti-macassared antiques as I had learned to do, using the turn-of-the-century bathroom carefully and quickly, and trying not to be unduly alarmed at the bust of a hedonistic-looking male ancestor of hers that inhabited the upstairs hall. Here was a head no viewer ever forgot—the frozen serpentine-like writhings of a beard, shoulder-length, plaster-of-Paris hair, with white, white eyes with no pupils to them. All this, the Gorgon-like statue featured, accentuated by an ever-burning, ever-flickering red vigil light.

"My Great Uncle Ed," Mrs. Decklebaum had explained to me the first time I passed him in the hall on the way to the linen closet. "His light never goes out," she had said. I could believe it.

From the short time I had spent with Mrs. Decklebaum I discovered that she used any and all of the symbols and icons, the representations and relics of all the great religions. The Star of David she prominently displayed from the window of her own upstairs bedroom and this could be seen a full two blocks away. The Hindu God Shiva occupied a place of honor alongside a concrete walk on the west side of her white clapboard house. A statue of St. Francis, then, rested plunk in the middle of her bird bath in the back yard, while a reclining Buddha acted as a doorstop of some sort for the sometimes swinging door between her kitchen and dining room. In addition to all of this, Mrs. Decklebaum could, on occasion, be seen frantically flinging salt over her shoulder, and again, at certain times be in evidence of producing a genuine rabbit's foot from her canyonous bosom when the occasion warranted it.

"You'll enjoy the festivities," she said, interrupting my thoughts. "Everyone does."

I had to admit that I was looking forward to it. I had carefully watched Centennial's prize-persimmon trees and those along the walks on the way to and from Sesqui. I also had seen them spurting up and out in sometimes extremely adverse conditions, defying the sand and the poor soil. I had seen them along roadsides that were fenced in and I had seen them in the open fields. Some rose out of ditches and some stood triumphantly atop scattered mounds. But wherever they were, I had taken note of the green forbidden fruit and later, the soft-hazed paradise of slowly-ripening, soft, deliciously-beckoning fruit. But I can truthfully say, I never plucked a persimmon. I just couldn't. Mrs. Decklebaum's warning that very first day had guided my daily thoughts and excursions. Why, I wasn't even tempted.

"What happens if a 'simmon doesn't fall?" Sandy had asked during science class one day.

"It hangs on into winter, then," the Science Encyclopedia had informed us, "as important food for foxes, racoons, opossums, skunks, ringtailed cats, and for birds." So there was reason to believe that a 'simmon did its duty, no matter if it let go or not.

"Mrs. Decklebaum," I found myself saying, "why don't you go ahead and use my room, too. I can sleep on the couch. That way, you could handle more guests."

"Why, bless you," Mrs. Decklebaum smiled. "That's mighty nice of you. That is an idea."

"I could make room for four that way, couldn't I?" she looked up from her pudding mix.

And so it was that Mrs. Decklebaum informed the Jaycees that she would take in four paying guests for the duration of the festival.

When one of Mrs. Decklebaum's guests turned out to be Miss Forester, the Greentree Community School System's art teacher, I thought of the cliche: "It's a small world!"

"Another Auntie took my room," explained Miss Forester as she came through the door with her assortment of boxes and recorders, "I really live just two blocks away," she smiled. With Miss Forester came her Grand Aunt Tilson, her Great Uncle Aimes and her ex-fiancé, Burton Tylacki, with a bag of horehound candy in tow. Great Uncle Aimes carried a small portable cage wherein lodged a parakeet.

"Couldn't get anyone to care for it," Grand Aunt Tilson apologized.

"Shop at Sears! Shop at Sears!" shrieked the bird.

"How do!" said the ex-fiancé.

"How do!" said Grand Aunt Tilson with her mouth in a kind of persimmon pucker.

"How do!" said Great Uncle Aimes, exposing his horehound drop.

This invasion of paying guests left me feeling like a slab of Swiss cheese that had been recently riddled by flying buckshot.

Never Pluck a Persimmon

"Say," said Miss Forester looking at me, "haven't I seen you some place before?"

"Yess—," I answered, "in Sesqui. You came to give me an art lesson."

"Oh-h-h-h yes," Miss Forester remembered. Then her eyes darkened in recollection. "How have things been?" she asked.

Before I could answer Mrs. Decklebaum interrupted: "Well, well, well...let's show you your rooms, now," and everyone scurried forth, picking up the boxes and suitcases and parakeet and recorders.

Mrs. Decklebaum, then, with her clucking sounds, hurried ahead to show her guests the wherewithal of things. And, when all the towels and bars of soap and rooms had been assigned and issued, Mrs. Decklebaum, intent on winning the Prize Persimmon Contest this year, disappeared once again into the innards of her immaculate kitchen to continue on with yet another batch of her "'Simmony-Delight" 'simmon pudding.

But it was not long before Grand Aunt Tilson decided to come down to see what Mrs. Decklebaum was about.

"You say you've entered the persimmon pudding contest nineteen years in a row?" the Grand Aunt probed, her nose coming ever closer to Mrs. Decklebaum's bowl.

"Yes," Mrs. Decklebaum answered, masking the 'simmon pulp with the well-worn wooden spoon, "but I've almost given up hope of winning," she added.

"What's wrong with your recipe?" the Grand Aunt persisted.

"Nothing's wrong with it," Mrs. Decklebaum defended, trying hard to concentrate in spite of her distracting paying guest. "It's a secret recipe. 'Been handed down."

"Handed down, eh? With a secret ingredient in it, eh?" the Grand Aunt kept it up.

Mrs. Decklebaum snapped down the spoon onto the sink counter, strode resolutely across the room and snatched suddenly at a lone piece of paper which had been lying unnoticed on the side board. Stuffing the paper into her blue rick-racked apron pocket she turned around to face Grand Aunt Tilson.

"Madame," Mrs. Decklebaum began, her bottom lip trembling, "please will you leave my kitchen? I cannot concentrate when you keep asking me questions. Vamoose." Mrs. Decklebaum had never been more serious in her entire life.

"Well...I...I never," the Grand Aunt began, "I just came down to ask if we—the four of us—might get together in your living room for a—a talk session. It's been a long time since we all seen one another."

The lines of Mrs. Decklebaum's face softened.

"Certainly," she agreed. "Do make yourselves at home. I'm sorry if I'm jumpy."

"'S all right," the Grand Aunt smiled a little. "I'm sure you've a right to cook in your own kitchen without bein' bothered. Me, though," the Grand Aunt continued, "I'd put in a secret ingredient. Might be the one thing you need to win." And with this unasked for advice, Grand Aunt Tilson went back upstairs to summon The Group.

Possibly because she regretted her previous irritability, possibly because she was curious as to the ways of her odd-assortment of guests, Mrs. Decklebaum, only a short time later, did leave her kitchen, wiping her hands somewhat timidly on her apron and joined Grand Aunt Tilson, Great Uncle Aimes, Miss Forester, and the ex-fiancé Burton in the living room.

It was extremely difficult, trying to correct a set of arithmetic papers upstairs in Mrs. Decklebaum's bedroom, where I could hear even the click of Uncle Aimes' false teeth to say nothing of the unusual talk.

"Sakes alive," Mrs. Decklebaum said, coming upon the four of them, who, I learned later, sat in a compact circle with their knees touching.

"Sh-h-h-h-h," Grand Aunt Tilson admonished, "we're asking the ouija board to tell us 'bout your recipe. Not the recipe, mind you, just 'bout it."

"What about my recipe?" Mrs. Decklebaum's voice sounded defensive.

"Come join us," Miss Forester chimed in, and, why not call the school teacher upstairs? We need her knees to help balance this, too," Miss Forester explained.

And so it was that I found myself a part of this esoteric congregation, concentrating on the occult.

"What's wrong with Mrs. Decklebaum's persimmon pudding recipe?" Grand Aunt Tilson asked the board as though she was talking to a neighbor over the back fence. My knees seemed to be touching those of Great Uncle Aimes.

"Well, really..." Mrs. Decklebaum was still on the defensive. In a matter of seconds something started to move besides Great Uncle Aimes' knees.

Never Pluck a Persimmon

"N" the board started to spell...
"O" called out Miss Forester as soon as the dial stopped...
"T" the ex-fiancé then exclaimed...
"H" Mrs. Decklebaum gasped...
"I" Grand Aunt Tilson affirmed...
"N" Great Uncle Aimes grunted...
"G" and the dial stopped...and stopped...and the board rested.

"Nothing!" reiterated Grand Aunt Tilson.
"Well, how come she never wins the blue ribbon then?" she shouted back at the board as though it had forgotten to wear its hearing-aid.
The dial, a straight, stiff-necked piece of steel remained stationary in spite of the fact that, I discovered, again, that Great Uncle Aimes' knees did not.
"What does her recipe need to win?" Grand Aunt Tilson tried a new twist. Now the dial started up suddenly and excitedly:

"L" the board started to spell...
"E" called out Miss Forester...
"M" the ex-fiancé exclaimed...
"O" Mrs. Decklebaum gulped...
"N" Grand Aunt Tilson affirmed...
"J" Great Uncle Aimes grunted...
"U" I called out, getting into the act...
"I" whispered Miss Forester...
"C" Mrs. Decklebaum re-gulped...
"E" Grand Aunt Tilson affirmed...and the dial rested!

"LEMON JUICE!" Grand Aunt Tilson announced grandly.
"Lemon juice?" Mrs. Decklebaum questioned, unbelievingly.
"So it's lemon juice is it?" Great Uncle Aimes heaved.
"Lemon juice!" Miss Forester exclaimed again, continuing: "Mrs. Decklebaum, have you finished mixing this batch of—of pudding—in the kitchen?"
"Why, no," Mrs. Decklebaum replied and she reached her hand into her apron pocket to retrieve her recipe and to possibly study how lemon

juice might conceivably become a part of the precious persimmon pudding recipe that had been handed down to her over two generations.

"But will lemon juice be acceptable to the author of this recipe,—Mrs. Decklebaum's Grandmother?" Miss Forester intoned spookily. "Can we be sure of this?"

"Well," began Grand Aunt Tilson, "my Grandmother Tilson was receptive to many, many things

"What does that have to do with my recipe?" Mrs. Decklebaum wanted to know.

"Nothing," Grand Aunt Tilson declared, a little hurt. "I'm just comparin'."

"Well," Miss Forester was at it again, "do you think lemon juice will fit into your recipe?" and the subject was back on the track.

Mrs. Decklebaum studied her well-worn, folded paper: "I...I think it might," she considered, "but I'm not sure..."

"We've got to be sure that whosoever's recipe this is—though—does approve of the addition of lemon juice," Great Uncle Aimes said, coming to life. "That is the most important consideration. The ancestor must approve and be satisfied. We can't tamper..."

"But how can you ever be sure of anything like this?" I got it out just as the jangle of the doorbell interrupted.

"Oh, dear!" Mrs. Decklebaum exclaimed all flustered—"That's probably the chairman of the Persimmon Pudding Committee here to take my batch for sellin' to the fair...and..."

And Mrs. Decklebaum left the room to answer the summoning bell.

Miss Forester was the first to take notice of the folded piece of paper which was left behind on the ouija board. Her fingers moved to it seconds after her eyes had made their discovery.

"I don't think you had better do that," I started to protest.

"Good grief!" Miss Forester was disgusted. "Here we're trying to help and...Can't you understand?"

"Miss Morrow! Miss Morrow!" it was Mrs. Decklebaum now, calling me to the hallway where she was conversing with the caller. "It's for you. It's Mrs. Jackson here to see if you'll help with the corn-butterin'."

"Coming!" I called back.

"Here—take it," Miss Forester was now offering me the recipe. "Take it if you don't trust us."

Never Pluck a Persimmon

"No," I said in a loud whisper. "That's not the point." And now I had to clear my throat. "Here I am an outsider, also—as well as you. Mrs. Decklebaum does not want any outsider to see or read her recipe. I don't want to read it. I don't want it. And you're to leave it right there—where Mrs. Decklebaum left it," and with this I backed my way from the room, my eyes watching the while. Miss Forester removed her hand then from the paper and put it quietly into her lap. She looked genuinely ashamed of herself.

"Yes?" I called to Mrs. Decklebaum as I joined her and Mrs. Jackson in the hall.

The next few moments are black, anguished scars seared in Greentree memories...

Mrs. Jackson stayed only three minutes, but three minutes that turned out to be an eternity.

When Mrs. Decklebaum and I rejoined the ouija group we beheld an exuberant Miss Forester coming downstairs into the living room.

"Mrs. Decklebaum!" she was almost shouting with happiness.

"The lemon juice will work out just fine. We can be sure."

"Sure without tryin' it first?" Mrs. Decklebaum's manner wasn't positive of anything.

"Positively!" Miss Forester added smugly, "the smoke went straight up."

"The smoke?" both Mrs. Decklebaum and I asked at the same time.

"The smoke from the recipe," Grand Aunt Tilson affirmed. "To be sure ancestors approve we always burn a thing to them if possible and if the smoke goes up, it's all hunky-dory. If it goes down,—well...we just forget about it. That's disapproval," she explained.

"You...burned...my persimmon recipe?" Mrs. Decklebaum choked it out.

"Yes," Miss Forester smiled. But the smile was gradually leaving her face. "At the vigil light in the hall...the one that's in front of that ancestor of yours..." Then she tried again: "The atmosphere was perfect, really."

By this time I clasped Mrs. Decklebaum's hand in a futile, mute kind of condolence.

"You don't have a copy, do you Mrs. Decklebaum?" I asked, groping for words.

"No copy," Mrs. Decklehaum sank into a lumpily-stuffed chair.

"But..." I felt it necessary to persist, "don't you know it by heart?"

"No" came the little thin answer. "I can never remember recipes,—I always have to keep lookin'..."

The sadness in the quaint living room settled down somberly now on all the living occupants. What Mrs. Decklebaum's ancestors were doing now I couldn't say, but even Great Uncle Aimes' knees had come to a halt.

One by one of the paying guests folded up a chair here—and the ouija board there, and quietly tip-toed up to their rooms, their handkerchiefs held up to their mouths to muffle in their feelings.

"I'm sorry," Miss Forester said in a whisper and she, too, ascended. Her ex-fiancé Burton, also extremely downcast, assisted her.

"I can't even finish the batch I've got out there in the kitchen," Mrs. Decklebaum lamented to me as I stroked her forehead with a piece of limp apron.

"I guess not," was all I could offer, knowing nothing of culinary matters.

And in a few more days all the bobbing for apples, and all the buttering of the corn, and all the awarding of prizes and the chicken dinners and the bouncing, happy children running, 'mid the tables and booths to the rollicking tunes from the calliope—all this was over and done with for another year. And Greentree had another winner in the Persimmon Pudding contest and another blue ribbon had been awarded. And when rumor had it that "a dash of lemon juice" had made all the difference in the world between previously-judged puddings and the winner's of this year's Persimmon contest—well, Mrs. Decklebaum whinnied a wisp of a sigh and said: "Well, dearie," and she inhaled again, "they say everything happens for the best. Do you believe that?"

"I don't know," I had to admit. "I don't know."

Perhaps it was so. Perhaps it might succeed in keeping Miss Forester away from Sesqui—hexed or not—since seeing me could only remind her of a painful experience. But what good could come from all this to Mrs. Decklebaum?

Questions had no answers, but, for better or for worse, the Fall Festival was over and Greentree could now settle down for its long winter nap with the persimmon sap now retreating into the ground where it would remain until spring—waiting again for those sunny days and happy times when dreams were tied and untied, woven and twisted, and delicately-fashioned, all in the guise of one solid, heavenly, blue-ribbon!

XI

A STAR IS BORN

It was on a snow-heavy, sleepy afternoon in late November that Sandy suggested I tell the class a story.

"All right," I agreed. "Let's push our chairs into a circle," and all the boys and girls complied. We needed the break as the phonics drill had tired us all out.

So, together we glided the desks and chairs over the lemony-beige rug. The circle formation gave a more relaxed atmosphere...it was cozy and...

But my hands froze in dumbfounded consternation! I had horrifyingly clutched a desk that had long sticky strands of "used" licorice chewing gum stuck beneath. The gum now adhered tenaciously to my quiverring fingers. Icy tingles chased one another up and down my spine like an elevator out of control while a wave of nausea encompassed my entire being.

"Children," I gulped, "I'll be right back," and in one leap I made straight for Centennial.

I held my arms out, airplane-style, afraid that my hands, oh, hideous hands, might contaminate the rest of me. What could be worse,—what could be more devastating, more spine-chilling, more nauseous to any teacher than to experience first-hand the wet wads of saliva-saturated chewing gum?

How I yearned for Centennial's hot, hot, clear water!

"We must get Sesqui connected," I said over and over again to myself as I ran. "We must get her running water!" It was a solemn promise to Sesqui and to myself.

And when at last the warm healing waters reached my tainted, tormented hands,—East had met West! Brother was brother! Lady MacBeth was made whole! Even Mr. Birly wasn't such a bad fellow after all.

But who was the little culprit over in Sesqui who was silently chewing, and then discarding in such a semi-public way?

"Children," I said quietly to my pupils on my return to Sesqui, "you must never, never, never, chew gum and place wads underneath the desks!

Now, I'm asking no questions, but whoever did stick all that licorice gum underneath that desk must never, never do it again."

"I would never do a thing like that," Henry Burnett declared, shaking his head disapprovingly.

"Of course you wouldn't," I acquiesced.

"No," Henry continued. "I always put mine in back of my ear underneath my haircut—so I can find it again when I want to chew it."

The class nodded understandingly and the story hour commenced.

The story of the day was "The Fisherman and His Wife" and I read to the beautifully expressive eager eyes and tried to forget all about sticking wads.

And when the Fisherman pleaded to the enchanted Fish:

> "O man of the Sea,
> Come, listen to me!
> Alice my wife,
> the bane of my life
> has asked me to beg a favor of thee!"
> I pleaded poignantly.

And as the story progressed, the sad tale about the greedy woman who was never satisfied with the many wonderful gifts the fish bestowed upon her, emerged. She had moved from a ditch to a cottage, from a cottage to a mansion, from a mansion to a castle, and from a castle to a palace and still she was not happy. So, when she had been crowned emperor and still was dissatisfied because she could not control the sun and the moon, she asked her husband again to go back to the fish for yet this new power. And when the fish finally got sick and tired catering to such a greedy individual and said:

> "All palaces and riches disappear!
> Go back to your ditch again!"

I looked around and saw nothing but confusion on the faces of my third-graders.

"That's a good story," said Henry, "all about a woman who moved a lot!"

"Is that what the story is about?" I asked.

Never Pluck a Persimmon

The class nodded.

"She moved too much," Sandy commented.

So, in order to give yet another example I began: "Suppose your Mother went to the bakeshop to buy doughnuts and when she got home you said: 'Ah-h-h-h why did you bring doughnuts? Why didn't you buy a chocolate cake?'

"And the next night your Mother went to the store again to get the chocolate cake and you said: 'Ah-h-h-h why didn't you bring a pecan pie home, too. I feel like a piece of pie tonight.'

"And," I continued, "when your Mother brought home the pecan pie the next evening you said: 'Ah-h-h-h I'd rather have had some toll house cookies—instead of pecan pie.'

"And the next night when your Mother brought the toll house cookies you said: 'Ah-h-h-h toll house cookies are okay but I would rather have had a chocolate-carrot cake.'

"And when your Mother brought the chocolate carrot cake you grumbled: 'Gee whiz—my mouth is watering for some good custard pie—not chocolate carrot cake.'

"Well, now," I finally concluded dramatically, "what would your Mother say?"

Unita was ready. Indignantly she raised her hand and then stood to give her comment. Pulling in her breath in short gasps she heaved out her chest, clenched her fists and said disgustedly: "Miss Morrow, my Momma would say: 'MAKE UP YOUR MIND!'"

"Well, class," I said, giving up in desperation, "let's get on with the acting out of the story now."

This was an exercise the children enjoyed immensely. By taking the various roles, by speaking out in class, imagination was developed, as well as diction, expression, articulation, memory, etc. But a knock came to Sesqui one afternoon about my assigning of parts.

It was Mr. Burnett, Henry's father, standing in the doorway.

"Miss Morrow," he began somewhat apologetically. "I don't like to complain, but Henry told me he is the tail on a comet in the Winter Pageant"

"Yes?" I affirmed, "but..."

"But, Miss Morrow," Mr. Burnett continued in his quiet, matter-of-fact tone, "so far Henry has been the hair in <u>Rapunzel</u>, the glass slipper in <u>Cinderella</u>, Toto in <u>The Wizard of Oz</u> and the bowl of porridge in

Goldilocks. You know that life is no bowl of cherries, but when you know your son is a bowl of porridge—well, it's a low blow.. and now..not even a comet, but a tail…"

"But…" I tried to interrupt.

"Now I have friends," he continued. "My friends have kids…"

"Mr. Burnett," I had trouble interrupting, "Henry volunteered to be the slipper...and the hair...and the bowl of porridge…"

"Come inside for a moment and let the children explain our WINTER PAGEANT to you," I beckoned to him.

Mr. Burnett entered Sesqui, cap in hand.

"Hi, Dad," Henry greeted his father.

Mr. Burnett nodded to his son and smiled.

Turning now to face the class I introduced Mr. Burnett, and then said, "Is there anyone here who would like to tell Mr. Burnett about the WINTER PAGEANT?"

Mary Jane's hand was the first up. Standing at her desk, she began: The WINTER PAGEANT will be a scientific kind of play. Planet—ah…Planetariums, all over the United States, every year, ah—ah—have shows explaining,—at Christmas time,—what might have happened in the sky,—when, ah…when, ah…" and here she took a deep breath…

…that very moment Henry came to life and shouted out: "WHEN THE WISE MEN FOLLOWED THE STAR TO BETHLEHEM!!"

Mary Jane nodded her approval to Henry and sat down.

"Thank you, Mary Jane,—and, of course, Henry," I offered to the volunteers.

To Sandy I directed, "Please go to the board now Sandy and draw the broomstar that the Chineses scientists talk about."

With chalk in hand, Sandy drew a comet with a very long tail,—that did resemble a kind of broom with a long handle. Turning now, to face the class, Sandy explained: "Around 5 B.C. Chinese scientists saw a comet in the sky that had a long, long tail, and this comet lasted in the sky for 70 days…"

Justin's hand began flapping now for attention. Sandy, turning to Justin, asked, "And, what about these 70 days?"

Smiling knowingly, Justin answered, "That was just enough time for the Wise Men to make it to Bethlehem." This comet became known years later as the Star of Bethlehem!" he finished off.

Never Pluck a Persimmon

Here, Sandy interrupts. "Yes," she began. "It's like a meeting of the three planets and so there is much light. And this had much meaning for the Magi, or the three Wise Men," she added.

Mr. Burnett was beaming. Turning to the upturned faces of the boys and girls, he said, "Wow! That was a great science lesson for me! Thank you for telling me all about the stars and planets" he concluded.

"See," said Henry to his father, "I'm a tail on this comet but I'm really the Star of Bethlehem!" Henry almost shouted to his father with glee. Mr. Burnett laughed back and hugged his son.

To Henry he said "You'll make a great Star of Bethlehem, son!," and then he was gone.: It was three days later when an exuberant Mr. Burnett returned.

"Say, Miss Morrow," he said excitedly, "you should see the costume! And—well, I've been thinking. Rather than have Henry just stand there and—and shine, well, the Star of Bethlehem moved, didn't it? The Wise Men followed it. Why couldn't Henry move across the stage—high up?"

"Well, that would be fine with me, but how could we work it?" I was puzzled.

"Leave it to me," Mr. Burnett said. "I've got an idea."

To my complete amazement Mr. Burnett did come up with something so unique that the Pyramid Builders of ancient Egypt would have been impressed. Each night after leaving his factory job Mr. Burnett came to Centennial and fiddled with ropes and levers, screw drivers and pulleys. His interest was commendable and Henry was so proud.

"Henry's going to be the star of the whole show," he'd say through a mouthful of nails. "Wait and see."

Dress rehearsal was held on a Sunday afternoon and I was surprised and pleased at the smooth run-through. Henry was simply magnanimous as he stood on the small platform that was connected by the pulleys and ropes. He was guided and glided across the stage as the reverent Wise Men dutifully followed. He was hoisted slowly along—always just ahead of them—up, up, at just the right height. It was truly ingenious! And how dramatic a moment when the Star halted just above the stable!

"Oh, Mr. Burnett, you've added so much to the play," I declared in sincere appreciation.

Mr. Burnett chuckled. He was pleased, too.

Came December 14 and once again a Greentree congregation gathered for a program. But this performance was no pep assembly nor a Michael Zig-Zaggle attempt. It was planned to call attention to Christmas, the sacred Christian feast. It was to be serious and profound. And if Henry had stayed the comet all might have been well. But, at the cue of "We Three Kings of Orient Are" from the piano, the curtains parted and Greentree was exposed to Henry Burnett—living Star!

Henry was on his platform where he belonged, but something was wrong. His costume, I noted, which was made of aluminum foil, shot out somewhat haphazardly in all directions—and it had been in place moments before. But now—now it gave the impression of a silver sun recently escaped from a solar asylum. And, Henry wasn't twinkling! He twangled! He had a bit of tinsel dangling here and white crepe paper streamers drooping there—and, I remembered too late—that Mr. Burnett had a history of drinking!

And so, without any warning to the staid townspeople of Greentree, the Star of Bethlehem shot up suddenly like a meteor in reverse, descended somewhat momentarily, and then streaked upward again, ever so jerkily, until it was completely out of sight! All this before the astounded eyes of the audience and the Wise Men! After dangling precariously in the Centennial stage heavens it swooped back to earth again, hovering at a height of one foot from the stage floor. Here the Star remained, an erratic yo-yo resting. But what King wants to look the Star in the eye?

Mr. Burnett possibly got this thought from his position behind stage at the controls, so he did something about it. While the piano plodded along its Oriental way, mirroring at times the consternation of the astounded populace, Henry was suddenly yanked up again and sent on his Milky Way. The Star now zoomed crazily to the Left of the stage—then to the Right. Then back to the Left again! The Wise Men, Robert Jackson, Randy Gibbs, and Carl Steward, darted this way and then that way until they stopped completely, utterly spent with the senseless activity. They ultimately just stopped dead to watch the show, too, their crowns at all angles on their heads, their robes in disarray from unkingly actions. They had been driven men but now they were watching a humdinger of a tennis match. They looked to the right and then to the left and they even saw the Star when it went out of bounds, having the edge on the Greentree audience.

Henry by this time had lost the perplexed look that he had carried on his face during his spasmodic movements. The Henry I could see was now developing into one chartreuse glow which the spotlight was baring each time it caught up with his frantic rushings. But, fortunately, Henry did seem to be slowing down. The music was also showing signs of letting up, and not a moment too soon.

The Star by this time was now directly over the stable! With some luck it could come down there—if Mr. Burnett would only...

"Miss Morrow," someone whispered urgently in my ear, "Stop that madman!"

It was Mr. Birly echoing my sentiments..But it was not necessary.

The platform came down smack-center on the flat stable almost soundlessly. A shaken Henry, however, but a still glimmering one, stumbled out of his air-borne prison.

The relieved piano player was now sounding her last chord and Henry was in the initial stages of a sweeping bow. He bent at the waist—his aluminum and cardboard crackling noisily as he went over.

"Thank God," Mr. Birly said decisively.

"But Henry wasn't supposed to be taking a bow," I started to think. The Three Kings were waiting, hands in pockets, for further developments.

The Star of Bethlehem then stepped thuddingly out of character, the same moment that Mary and Joseph chose to peek out a stable window with expressions of "Wha' happened?" on their faces. Clutching a scraggly tree prop for support, Henry Burnett, Star of Bethlehem, then, suddenly, emphatically, uncontrollably, decisively, threw up before the witnessing eyes of Greentree's citizenry

> on the roof of the stable—
> on the stage of Centennial—
> In this year of Our Lord.

XII

THE SCIENCE FAIR

My concern for Henry, after the Star fiasco, was mental anguish wasted. Had the boy been a more sensitive child perhaps, the experience of being plummeted around in public would have been something from which he never would have recovered. But to Henry, it was a rich kind of metamorphosis. The lowly caterpillar had flown while the whole world watched. Henry was now important. He was Greentree's Peter Pan, a hero with wings! And how he loved every minute of it.

People said: "How goes it, Henry?" and "Hi, Henry, how are you?" and things like, "You stay out of flying saucers now."

And so it was Henry and not Robert Jackson who became Michael Zig-Zaggle personified. For the citizens of Greentree all remembered that here was the boy—the third grader—who was one of "those" who, because of crowded conditions, was forced to go to school in a unique kind of building that had no connections. In this way, then, Henry did much for the cause.

The School Board Members who stood for Sesqui, John Calhoun Jones and Mrs. Cynthia Jefferson Davis, alternated in inviting Henry and his mother and father to dinner occasionally. So, the light from one errant star had helped to focus attention on deprived Sesqui, and Greentree was the richer for it.

But while Mr. Jones and Mrs. Davis were arousing the town to the needs of Sesqui, Mr. Webster and Mr. Clay, the remaining Board members, saw no need to give Sesqui "extra" privileges or to cater to Sesqui-ites in any way.

Centennial and Sesqui were really one and the same thing they said—one inseparable Union—and one was not to be interposed one before the other. Therefore, they said, Centennial and Sesqui, with no inconvenience whatsoever, could continue to use the same toilet facilities.

Strangely enough things bubbled to a boiling point at Centennial's annual Science Fair. The Science Fair was a big-enough thing in itself without political overtones. There was always, I understood, an effervescent breathlessness on the part of some scientific devotees for this yearly occasion. After all, there were blue ribbons to be had, and prestige,

Never Pluck a Persimmon

and prestige in Greentree was a bigger thing than a Goodyear dirigible in a pollywog pond. This enthusiasm was reflected in my third graders as they planned for the Fair: "I'm bringing in a bird-egg tree," said Audubon-backer Randy.

"I'm bringing in a whole hatchery. My chicken eggs will hatch by that date," Unita put in.

"I'm making soap," said Sandy.

But some of the proposed projects were discarded at the request of Mr. Birly who exhorted a wary censorship over the submissions.

"The Bees and the Birds and then Some" and "Applied Psychology to an Ant Hill" were eliminated.

"What third-grader could invent a project like that on his own?" Mr. Birly was exasperated. I hated to tell him.

"The Excretory System of a Dinosaur" was also discarded for apparent reasons.."

Accepted were: "A Study of the Praying Mantis—Praying", "The Penguin Egg—Unhatched", "My Grandmother's Gallstones—Jarred", "A Weather Map—with Predictions" and of course "The Bird-Egg Tree," "The Hatchery," and "Grandmother's Old-Fashioned Soap."

Unfortunately, the penguin egg was brought in two days before the deadline and was placed on the science table, sardined between an elephant's tusk, a bird's nest, an active framed ant colony, a sectioned-out piece of dried manure and a few random fish skeletons. While the egg had a comparatively safe resting place atop a cupped paper-elevation, it nevertheless was jarred from its perch and fell to the floor where it remained unnoticed until Sandy came up quietly to whisper: "Miss Morrow. I think Robert Jackson should go to Centennial."

I looked over at Robert who was busily finishing his arithmetic problems. He was very much unconcerned if what Sandy said was true.

But Henry Burnett broke the silence of the room: "Miss Morrow," he said, holding his nose, "there is an awful smell comin' from that egg there."

A rotten penguin egg! In a matter of seconds all the perfumes of Arabia were suddenly reversed.

And Mary Jane was in tears!

"How can I enter the Science Fair?" she pleaded. "My Dad brought me that from the Navy only a year ago—and now it's...it's cracked! And it smells so-o-o-o bad," she sobbed.

"I think we can tape it together," I quieted her. "The judges are very understanding." I hoped also that their noses were numbed nuances of smelling and I lamented the fact that her father had not seen fit to leave penguin eggs for the penguins.

"You'll see, Mary Jane," I assured her. "Everything will turn out all right."

But what an addle-brained optimist I turned out to be!

When I entered the Centennial gymnasium there was an undefinable zing to the air. Everything was in animation. The people were moving in and out among the exhibits. Some of the exhibits themselves were moving and something above everyone's heads was parading! Signs! Lots and lots of them. In an age of demonstrators Greentree was proving to be no exception.

Beside the exhibit "The Praying Mantis—Praying" the signs were:

HOW COME <u>HE</u> CAN, AND THE SUPREME COURT SAYS <u>I</u> CAN'T?
and
SO! AND IN A PUBLIC SCHOOL, TOO!

Near an exhibit explaining the anatomy of a vulture were signs:

WHAT GREENTREE CAN DO TO ATTRACT BUZZARDS

and near the sewing room:
THE COLOR PERSIMMON IS FIRST IN FALL FASHIONS
and
HOW TO LOSE WEIGHT ON A PERSIMMON DIET!

But what particularly caught my eye were the numerous placards deploring Sesqui's condition in a modern world:

**WITHOUT CONNECTIONS...
WITHOUT FACILITIES...
WITHOUT RESULTS...SESQUI**

WHO'S SUFFERING AT SESQUI? __ONLY THE KIDS!

LET'S PUT ON END TO MICHAEL ZIG-ZAGGLE!

THE KNOWLEDGE OF KNOWING THERE IS NONE…IS TOO MUCH!

ZIGGLES AND ZAGGLES HAVE NO PLACE IN PUBLIC EDUCATION!

Even though the scientific displays had been judged by educators from a neighboring township and the blue ribbons already awarded, (Sandy had one for her recipe of Grandma's Old-Fashioned Soap, complete with sample bars)—I noted little interest in them.

The politicians and not the scientists were carrying the day. Over in one corner, Mr. Clay, mounted on an empty case of soda-pop, was answering questions to a group of parents:

"Sesqui and Centennial's relationship with one another is of utmost importance not only to the existence of our school system but to the well-being of mankind," I could hear him saying.

At the stage side of the gymnasium there were more signs:

SESQUI HAS RIGHTS TOO!

SESQUI WILL FIGHT!

SESQUI **WILL BE CONNECTED!**

It was Henry Burnett who stood smiling happily on this side, along with Mr. John Calhoun Jones, President of the School Board, who was now declaring in loud tones:

"Connect Sesqui and you will forever settle the questions at issue.. You will save the Union that exists between Centennial and Sesqui. But, can this be done? Yes, easily—but not by the weaker party for it can of itself do nothing—not even protect itself—but by the stronger. Centennial and the entire School Board has only to will it to accomplish it!" And here Mr. Jones took a deep breath.

"There should be no difficulty in devising a provision to provide Sesqui with the necessities of life!" he continued, "the provision will protect Sesqui, but it will also improve and strengthen Centennial instead of impairing and weakening her!"

And then he sang out loudly and clearly:

"If you who represent the people of Greentree cannot agree to settle things on the broad principle of justice and duty for Sesqui—say so here and now or Sesqui will have to take things into her own hands!" And here Mr. John Calhoun Jones paused while his audience clapped enthusiastically.

But suddenly a dark figure with unruly hair and unpressed pants stepped from the crowd.

"Mr. President," he said in clear, somber tones, "may I speak?"

Mr. Jones smiled and said benevolently:

"Free speech is part of America," he replied, "and an integral part of Greentree!"

And Mr. Webster, prominent Greentree manufacturer and School Board Member who opposed Sesqui's being connected took the podium.

"Mr. President," he began, "I should much prefer to have heard from every member on this floor declarations of the opinion that the Union between Centennial and Sesqui could never be dissolved than declaration of opinion that in any case, under the pressure of circumstances such a dissolution was possible.

"I say a voluntary separation with alimony on one side and on the other would be preposterous. Where is the flag of Centennial and Sesqui to remain? Where is the eagle still to tower? Or is he to cower and shrink, and fall to the ground?" Mr. Webster's voice rang with passion and conviction as more and more people joined the group to listen:

"Why, sir, our ancestors—our fathers and grandfathers—those of them that are yet living amongst us with prolonged lives—would rebuke and reproach us—and our children and our grandchildren would cry out, 'Shame on us!' if we of this generation should dishonor those ensigns of the power of the School Board and the harmony of the Union which exists between Centennial and Sesqui.

"And now, Mr. President," and here Mr. Webster turned to John Calhoun Jones, "instead of speaking of the possibility or utility of taking things into your own hands—instead of groping with those ideas so full of all that is horrid and horrible—instead of dwelling in these caverns of darkness,—let us enjoy the fresh air of liberty and union—let us come out into the light of day—let us cherish those hopes which belong to us—let us devote ourselves to those great objects that are fit for our consideration and our action,—let us raise our conceptions to the magnitude and the importance of the duties that devolve upon us—let our comprehension be as broad as the country for which we act, our aspirations as high as its certain destiny—let us not be pigmies in a case that calls for men." And Mr. Webster bowed his head.

The applause was a thunderous ovation. But then Mrs. Davis pushed her way to the podium. It was apparent by now that the Science Fair had gone by the board and Sesqui and her problems were carrying the day.

Mrs. Cynthia Davis, Mrs. Cynthia Jefferson Davis, extended her arms for silence and began in moderate tones which gradually reached piercing, crescendo proportions.

"Ladeez and Gentlemen," she began, "if present conditions at Sesqui prevail, I propose to show how the Union between Centennial and Sesqui *cannot* be saved. It cannot be saved by eulogies on this Union however splendid or numerous. The cry of 'Union, Union, the glorious Union' can no more prevent disunion than the cry of 'Health, Health, glorious Health' on the part of the physician can save a patient lying dangerously ill." Here Henry Burnett clasped his hands above his head in affirmation and the audience paused to laugh and clap. Mrs. Davis continued:

"Sesqui upholds the principle of self-determination and self-government," Mrs. Davis pronounced profoundly.

"In the exercise of a right so ancient," she continued, "so well-established and so necessary for self-preservation, the people of Sesqui—the parents of Sesqui-ites, I should say, determined that the wrongs which they had suffered and the evils with which their children were menaced, required that they should pass recommendations stating their fundamental rights. Sesqui is organizing—functions of executive, legislative and judicial magistrates to handle these grievances that are beginning to materialize."

Then in prophetic, resounding tones Mrs. Davis declared:

"Sesqui-Centennial cannot endure permanently half-connected and therefore half-free!" And here Mrs. Davis bowed profusely and then sat down midst the wild cheering that followed her statements.

It was at this point that a local plumber—accompanied by Mr. Jackson—began passing literature about the costs—real and hidden—of connecting Sesqui. It was apparent that the citizenry, including local merchants, were taking things into their own hands. But on the fringe of the crowd a tall, dark gaunt figure of a man raised his hand.

"May I say something?" the stranger asked in a loud, warm, resonant voice.

Mrs. Davis put her hand up for the plumber to stop his proceedings.

"Yes?" she asked of the man.

"I would like to say just one thought," he continued, somewhat embarrassed.

"Of course," she encouraged. "Would you come to the podium?"

The tall man looked as though he had trouble with ready-made suits. His shirt cuffs were in full evidence as they swung from his coat sleeves as he walked slowly to the stage.

"Friends and citizens of Greentree," he began, gesturing with his long thin hands. "Physically-speaking Sesqui and Centennial cannot separate. We cannot remove our respective schools from each other nor build an impassable wall between them. A husband and wife may be divorced and go out of the presence and beyond the reach of each other, but Sesqui and Centennial cannot do this. They must remain face to face and intercourse, either amicable or hostile, must continue between them. But I do have a solution," he added.

Then, his voice ringing with assurance, he declared:

"I say—intelligence—patriotism—common sense—and a firm reliance on Him who has never yet forsaken this favored town of Greentree are still competent to adjust in the best way all our present difficulties!" And the tall man had finished. As he returned to his place in the audience the crowd respectfully formed a kind of guard of honor to usher him back. He was however patted profusely on his back and cheered by some, but there were others who stood sullen in their thoughts. They appeared unconvinced of the tall man's words.

It was certainly a complicated problem. It was hard to understand how such a small thing as a tiny, modern portable classroom parked thirty feet from a huge stationary edifice of community pride,—with a persimmon grove between—could divide a town to this extent. But the P.T.A. Committee, headed by the Jacksons, proved itself a formidable minority group. And it was true. This minority group was slicing the town into two distinct camps. You almost chose your friends now, according to which side they favored.

It was at this moment that I caught sight of Mr. Birly. He was scratching his head and shifting his weight from one foot to another. Anyone could see he was a torn man. Should Sesqui be connected to the plumbing lines of Centennial or should it remain unconnected? Was it a permanent enough thing to be attached permanently even if the Board did come up with the money? And, if not connected, well then, the persimmon trees done away with...? Here was indecision. Here was a certain kind of anguish. Who could say which was the proper path to pursue?

"Well," I thought, "if the principal of this Union—of Sesqui and of Centennial,—was confused, well,—wasn't everyone?"

XIII

THE CLOTHING DRIVE

"The clothing drive will be held all week long," I announced to the class as directed via a Special Bulletin from Mr. Birly. "You are to bring shoes, sweaters, pants, jeans, pajamas, underwear, blankets, suits, overshoes, dresses and diapers," I quoted from the circular. "We will send the entire collection to needy people in Tintown, U.S.A."

"What about my mother's wedding dress?" Sandy wanted to know.

"No," answered Henry, "it's not warm."

"What about a negligee?" Justin asked.

"No, that's not warm either," I replied, taking the cue from Henry.

"What is a negligee?" Carl asked, his hand raised.

"A negligee is a woman's dressing gown," I answered.

"But it's not for dressing, is it?" Mary Jane asked, her head tilted.

"Let's get back to the clothing drive now. We're all supposed to bring in good used clothing—not rags."

"What about drawers?" Unita asked without raising her hand.

"Drawers are fine," I found myself answering.

"And," I continued, "the class who brings in the most—by weight—will win a prize. We'll weigh the clothing on the nurse's scale over in Centennial."

"What will the prize be?" Justin asked.

"Mr. Birly will tell us what it is later," I answered.

"It's probably a cake," declared Sandy. "A chocolate one."

"Maybe it will be rest rooms, "speculated one-track-mind Robert Jackson, "if Sesqui wins."

"Let's not think about the prize but about helping the poor people of Tintown," I put in. "Tintown is suffering from much unemployment. Tintown needs our help. Tintown is a coal mining town but the mines have been closed. So, let's fill a bag for them with our good used clothes. I've heard that school children will not be able to get to school there if you fail them. They depend on this drive each year," and the children nodded their heads and we went back to our arithmetic concepts.

And the clothing dribbled in—a pair of socks here, an undershirt there. We were contributing almost nil to Tintown, U.S.A. What could I do to stir them up?

But then Justin Mackin came forward.

"Miss Morrow," he began in his innocent way, "my Father wants to know if I can bring in some men's suits—for the clothing drive."

This wouldn't be helping the kids but maybe it would help their fathers get out of the house to look for some other work.

"Certainly," I cried, "certainly!"

"Well they're awful heavy—each one weighs between two and three lbs. alone," he continued.

"Oh, wonderful weight!" I thought.

But I said:

"Fine. Fine. The heavier the better!" and I was thankful that Sesqui just might make a mark on this clothing drive.

"Will tomorrow after school be a good time?" Justin kept the conversation open.

"Fine. I'll be here 'til four," I replied.

"Well...my Father will bring the car then," Justin finished.

"Very good," I encouraged. "I'll be waiting."

What I didn't realize was that when Mr. Mackin promised to bring the car he meant it. When he promised to bring men's suits—he meant that, too. And when he said four o'clock—that's what Mr. Mackin meant.

At precisely four the very next afternoon the roar of an engine came precariously close to Sesqui.

"Wha..." I started to say to myself. But I looked up from my Plan Book in time to glimpse an enormously finned red Cadillac streaking across the Centennial lawn—to Sesqui—to me!

"On the lawn! The grass! Thank God the petunias were gone! Oh, if Mr. Birly sees..." I mentally anguished.

"Hi there, Miss Morrow," Mr. Mackin introduced himself from the car. "I'm Mr. Mackin!"

"How do you do, sir," I said from Sesqui's doorway.

"Hello, Justin," I added, seeing the small blonde hair coming from behind Mr. Mackin's enormous front.

"We've brought the suits!" Mr. Mackin said as he alighted from the car. "We drove over the lawn and—well, it would be too complicated otherwise. We've got seventy-six suits here!"

"Seventy-six!" I could hardly comprehend such a number. "You couldn't have grown out of seventy-six suits!" I said something I should have thought more about beforehand.

"No," Mr. Mackin laughed jovially. "I have a tuxedo rental agency. These are simply out of style now. They're good suits, though," he added, pleased with himself.

"Where shall we put them?" he asked, spying the outsides of the cedar-lined closets at the same time.

"You can begin there," I said weakly, wondering if he should start to unload. "I'll help."

"But should Mr. Mackin bother to unload?" I was befuddled. "Seventy-six tuxedos in Tintown are seventy-six tuxedos. And whatever for?"

"Mr. Mackin," I started wildly. "What would you have done with these—these tuxedos—if the Clothing Drive hadn't come along?"

"Well, now," Mr. Mackin was pensive. "Last time I found myself in a situation like this—'bout ten years ago—I had some pretty worn ones. When they rent 'em they don't take too good of care of them, ya know. Well, I just put them in the incinerator—but I thought this time..."

"You thought correctly," I said aloud, thinking that my dear old Irish Grandmother would have said "You did rightly."

"Put the tuxedos in the closets until we run out of space. By that time I'll think of something," I finished.

And Mr. Mackin, Justin and myself started hauling until we were interrupted by a lone, disheveled figure looming on the lawn in the semi-twilight.

"Here! Here!" Mr. Birly said in a half-shout, his tie flying, "what's the meaning of this? This is good grass. Not cement. Miss Morrow, is that you?"

"Mr. Birly," I said mustering calmness, "this is Mr. Mackin—Justin's father. He's bringing clothing for the Clothing Drive."

"Oh, I see, Mr. Birly said cordially, "how do you do?"

"How do," Mr. Mackin acknowledged.

"It's very heavy clothing, Mr. Birly," I continued my line of appeasement "that's why..."

"Tut, tut," Mr. Birly dismissed the stark-red-Cadillac that was sinking by the second into precious, still-greenish, dampish Centennial grass.

"May I help?" and he motioned toward the car.

I shot a desperate look to the red-leathered insides of the automobile, happily discovering that all the tuxedos were boxed, and thus hidden from Mr. Birly's all-seeing, avant-garde eyes.

Box after box was carried to Sesqui by Mr. Birly, Mr. Mackin, Justin and myself. It was finally Mr. Mackin who suggested:

"Perhaps we'd better hang some now. They all have hangers inside the boxes..."

"Perhaps we'd better," I agreed dreadingly, "but, on second thought," I was suddenly inspired, "why don't we stack these somewhere else—where there's room?"

"Fine," Mr. Birly complied. "How about over in my office?"

"No sooner said than done," Mr. Mackin shot back before any of us could say 'Sesqui-Centennial'! And so we drove back across the lawn to unload.

"Gee, we're not allowed to walk on the grass, but riding on it is fun," Justin commented.

"How did you ever collect all this clothing?" Mr. Birly asked the inevitable. "It must have taken years."

"Hardly..." Mr. Mackin answered from behind the wheel. "When they're out of style there's not much I can do with them. The kids just won't rent 'em if they're not the latest." Mr. Mackin had a mouth almost as enormous as his stomach.

"The kids?...Rent them?" Mr. Birly's confusion was apparent.

"The tuxedos. I'm in the Tuxedo Rental Business," Mr. Mackin stated as though he had just said "The earth is pear-shaped and you better believe it!"

However, it was not a pear that Mr. Birly resembled at this moment. It was more like a ripe tomato. As his face reddened he asked incredulously:

"Mr. Mackin...are...are there tuxedos in these boxes?"

"Yep," Mr. Mackin answered proudly. "Seventy-six of them. All in good condition, too, but a little too much padding in the shoulders...and those lapels..."

"Mr. Mackin," Mr. Birly said his name, straight-from-the-shoulder-like. "What is Tintown, U.S.A. going to do with seventy-six tuxedos? No one has a job there. There is no place to go in Tintown," and he broke off, but not before I noted a stifled sob to his usual booming baritone.

"Gee," Mr. Mackin said reflectively, "I never thought of that."

"They're nice and warm and Miss Morrow said..." Justin began.

"That's enough, Justin," I rescued myself.

"Well, in that case," Mr. Mackin seemed crestfallen, "I'll take them and burn them in my incinerator. I only thought..."

"Mr. Mackin," I put in. "Let's not be hasty. Now we don't know if Tintown can use them or not...this clothing."

"We've got a pretty good idea, though," Mr. Birly had to get his two-pence in.

"Why not wire Tintown and ask them?" I thought my idea had merit.

"How can you read from a wire?" Justin questioned, concerned.

"We'll discuss it later," I hushed him.

"Well...well..." Mr. Birly started to say.

By this time Mr. Mackin had lit up a cigar.

"I'll pay for the wire," he answered Mr. Birly's hesitation.

"All right," Mr. Birly agreed.

"But..." Mr. Mackin was driving a bargain now. "I've gone to all the trouble of packin' these suits. Suppose we unload the rest of these in your office and if Tintown doesn't want 'em *you* burn 'em in *your* incinerator."

"Fair enough," Mr. Birly finished off as Mr. Mackin, Mr. Birly, Justin and myself began the additional unloading.

With a resigned shrug of his now haunched shoulders, Mr. Birly picked the top box off the pile from the back seat of the red Cadillac.

He seemed to be asking himself:

"How explain *this* to the Superintendent?"

But he need not have concerned himself.

Two days later the answering telegram, which he generously shared with me, proclaimed:

    TUXEDOS ARE WELCOME IN TINTOWN STOP
    MANY USES STOP
    MANY THANKS
    SIGNED—JOHN CARLSON, MAYOR,
    PRESIDENT, CARLSON FUNERAL ESTABLISHMENT
    TINTOWN, U.S.A.

XIV

A.G.H.A.S.T.!

And one day I had a caller from Centennial. "I've been meaning to stop over to say hello," Miss Seward, fourth grade teacher from Centennial began, "but you know how busy we all are—over there," she added, nodding toward my Gargantuan better-half.

I nodded also, unable to speak. I was astounded at the woman's other-world appearance. Miss Seward was Miss Havisham minus the veil and bridal flowers. It was evident, however, that she had seen the sun but that she had never acknowledged it. True, her clock had stopped at twenty minutes to nine but her alarm was still pulled out.

"I've come to see if you'll join our wonderfully active Teachers' Association." she got right to the point.

"Oh?" I asked, having given no thought to any teacher organization thus far.

"I represent A.G.H.A.S.T.," she began. "I'm the Building Representative."

"A.G.H.A.S.T.?" I asked, uncomprehending.

"A.G.H.A.S.T.!" she repeated. Then she pursed her lips in a kind of I-believe-in-the-PROPER ALMIGHTY!—Proper dress, proper diet, proper education, proper... "Association of Grade & High American School Teachers!" she said directly and emphatically, unpursing her lips.

"A.G.H.A.S.T.!" I repeated, partially comprehending.

"We represent seventy percent of our teachers," she continued proudly. "We work for the teachers, for salaries, for fringe benefits—for many things," she stated, convinced of A.G.H.A.S.T.'s and her own worth. "We would like you to join us," she continued, "But first, we'd like you to join us in a cup of tea!" Miss Seward explained.

"Our annual membership drive culminates with a Tea Party—a very fancy tea party this coming Sunday afternoon," she added smirkingly, raising her eyebrows and pursing her lips again. "And—," she added, smirking again, "we'd like you to come."

"I wouldn't miss it," I said aloud. Miss Seward, having made her pitch, departed while I carefully marked my calendar. I had my first invitation! And in Greentree!

From the moment I entered the Centennial gymnasium that sunshiney Sunday afternoon I discerned that this Association really meant business. A.G.H.A.S.T. was actually in the process of serving not punch, not juleps, not coffee—but honest-to-goodness, unadulterated tea!

"How-do!" Miss Seward greeted me with her alarm still pulled out. She then proceeded to make me feel at home by introducing me to other members of august A.G.H.A.S.T. who were succulently sipping small samples of savory, scintillating tea.

"M-m-m-m-m-m-m-m—so you're the one who has been banished to Sesqui!" one woman laughed. "It's difficult teaching under such conditions I would imagine. But stay with it," she continued, "we all have to work ourselves up—and out—," she finished cheerfully.

"It's too bad Sesqui is not connected," said another, "but then we all have to put up with something difficult at times."

"What would we do without connections?" piped another, amused at her wit.

"You know, though, A.G.H.A.S.T. has already made up its mind," said one woman confidentially nodding..

"Made up its mind?" I did not understand.

"Even though we want your membership," her eyes glowed in their sockets, "we will not back having Sesqui connected. We believe things should stay as they are."

"You mean spare the persimmon trees—leave Sesqui thirty feet away from Centennial," I prompted sarcastically, "and let the chips fall where they may?" From the sudden substantial drop of her chin I wondered if I had pronounced chips correctly.

"Really..." she began, puffing up, "those simmon trees have been a vital part of Centennial long before any Sesqui arrived on the academic scene..."

Before I could come up with a retort Miss Seward rejoined the conversation:

"We have petit-fours," she pursed. "Let's go get some. And I was whisked away from this upsetting circle before my composure completely deserted.

Suddenly, Mr. Birly was at my side.

"Miss Morrow," he smiled, "I'd like you to meet my wife."

"How do you do," I nodded to the bespectacled pleasant-looking woman.

"Bertha! How good to see you!" said an apparent Birly-acquaintance, coming from behind.

"Bertha Birly!" I thought, wondering about her maiden name. "It shouldn't happen to anyone."

Everyone was smiling, shaking heads and hands simultaneously.

"Miss Morrow is the teacher over in Sesqui," Mr. Birly found it necessary to explain.

"Oh-h-h-h-h-h," said Mrs. Birly. Ane then she added, "Have you joined the Association yet?"

"No," I answered, "I haven't joined anything yet."

"Well stay away from G.O.T.!" said the woman who interrupted our group and who remained unintroduced.

"G.O.T.?" I questioned her.

"Greentree's Organized Teachers! The Union!" she said disgustedly.

At that moment a tinkling of a glass reminded everyone that the President of A.G.H.A.S.T. had not yet expressed her thanks to the cookie committee.

"Ladeez—Ladeez—and Gentlemen," she tapped again. And then the teacher who had selected the petit-fours stood for acclamation. Then the teacher who supplied the money with which to select the petit-fours, the Treasurer, stood. Finally, the teacher who placed the petit-fours onto the circular tray stood for her due. And then Mr. Birly was called to speak.

"We've got a special project to fulfill this year," he began, showing his teeth, "and it has to do with Sesqui."

"Since I'm the Principal of this (a little laugh) 'pipsqueak' school—along with Centennial of course, I've been asked to tell you all about it." And he paused for effect.

"We the Association have been asked—by our wonderful Superintendent Holmes," he was spreading it on, "to participate in a dedication ceremony. Sesqui is to be dedicated Sunday, February 1, in the evening," he added, showing his teeth again. "Now we'll have to think of something to do—to perform—for this occasion," and he looked beseechingly at his audience. "Would anyone have a suggestion?" he implored.

"Why can't our A.G.H.A.S.T. Glee Club sing for a change?" "They never do anymore!" put in one woman.

"Everyone knows the reason," answered another woman. "We have no uniforms!"

"What's a Glee Club without uniforms!" commented another, her lower lip dropping three inches. "The women members all broke down and bought or made themselves black gowns, but the men refused to go out and buy tuxedos," she continued pouting.

Mr. Birly's hair line ascended heavenward.

"How many male members belong to A.G.H.A.S.T.'S Glee Club?" he asked the woman, inspired.

"Fifty men, twenty-five women," she gave the vital statistics.

"Only fifty...wel-l-l-l-l-l," and Mr. Birly—turned and looked me squarely in the face.

The horror of it all suddenly seized me convulsively.

"Those tuxedos belong to Tintown," my eyes were saying frantically, "they're to be shipped tomorrow."

"There could be a slight delay," Mr. Birly said to me aloud. Calculatingly, he shook his head up and down, up and down.

"Yes," he said to the audience now, "perhaps the A.G.H.A.S.T. Glee Club will sing at the dedication," he rubbed his palms in satisfaction.

"Go back to your tea cups," he beamed now, glad that another problem had been solved.

"Mr. Birly," I said, rushing to him moments later, "You can't give those tuxedos to A.G.H.A.S.T. Those people in Tintown are expecting them!"

"Miss Morrow," he said, as simply as though he were stating a fact, "the people who will be wearing those tuxedos will never be aware of it. We'll send them on to Tintown, of course, but *after* the dedication."

"But," I argued, seeing that his mind was already made up, "suppose the men won't want to wear those out-of-date things?"

"A.G.H.A.S.T. men do what they are told to do," he settled the matter once and for all.

"When do we start rehearsing?" the woman who had started it all beamed at ingenious Mr. Birly.

"I'm alto," she said, as though there could be any question about it.

Dejected, I turned back to my prim, proper petit-four. I could suddenly see it as it really was,—a bit soggy around the edges and its roses dissolving into non-entities by the minute.

"So this is A.G.H.A.S.T.!" I thought, alarmed by my first exposure to the Association of Grade and High American School Teachers. "Whatever must G.O.T. be like?"

XV

G.O.T.—Greentree's Organized Teachers

Mr. Herendeen, coach-of-all-sports at Centennial, nailed me about G.O.T. the very next after-school afternoon.

"'Smighty nice place ya got here," he proferred. "I've never been in Sesqui before."

"It is pretty, isn't it?" I replied.

Mr. Herendeen was a big hulk of a man—reddish face, mammoth shoulders, baggy pants.

"I'll come to the reason for my visit," he leveled.

"Come to our beer party Friday night," he invited enthusiastically. "Look us over. See if you'd like to join the Union. We've looked you over and think you've got grit putting up with Sesqui not being connected. Such a waste!" and he looked around again.

"Beer," I protested. "But I don't drink beer. I'm allergic to it."

From the look on Mr. Herendeen's face I might have said: "I have an inoperable cancer."

"We usually carry creme soda," he came up with. "But beer is symbolic to the Union," he continued. "It is the Union, in a way."

And then he said in an exasperated tone:

"If you can't *feel* beer—the foam—taste it—dig it—understand it—enjoy it—how can you teach?" He was incredulous.

"I see what you mean," I answered, somewhat confused.

"Ya gotta *penetrate* living. *Dig* it." Then he asked abruptly: "Will ya come?"

"Yeah. I sure will," I responded, realizing that both A.G.H.A.S.T. and GOT had much to offer a fledgling teacher. "I wouldn't miss it."

"That's the spirit," he replied. "S'long. We'll be looking for you." And he walked back over the lemony beige rug and out the door.

What I actually expected from G.O.T.'s beer party I can't quite say, but what actually developed there has been categorized under the 'nightmare' area of my brain.

A private club—a private room in a private club, Hernando's Hideaway, to be explicit, accommodated G.O.T. that night.

"C'mon in," Mr. Herendeen greeted me as I was shown to a door by a waiter. "I won't tell Mr. Birly you came," he added jokingly.

The room was filled with what must have been all of the 30% of the Greentree teacher population which made up G.O.T. I judged the membership to ninety percent men, ten percent women.

"If all the new teachers would join G.O.T.," said one solicitous young man, "it'd stand for somethin'. It would mean that the young people were tired of the Mickey Mouse tactics of the Association."

"But the young people—the new teachers—" I corrected, "don't know enough about either organization—yet," I put in.

"Look," he said, moving his eyebrows in for the kill and giving me a whiff of famous G.O.T. beer, "level with me now. Do you plan to go places in your job?"

"What do you mean go places?" I asked.

"Do you want to be a principal?" he was more explicit.

"Why, no," I was astounded. "I don't ever plan to be a principal."

"Well then," he was relieved, "join G.O.T. You've got nothing to lose."

"By the way," he added, on second thought, "I'm Jebb Hinchey. I teach Machine Shop over at Harrison High."

"And I'm Virginia Morrow," I smiled, "I teach a third grade class in Sesqui—the little chicken coop of Centennial's." We both laughed.

"Would ya like your creme soda now?" Mr. Herendeen interrupted, a thin nervous-looking bottle in his hand.

"Thank you," I smiled, and Jebb Hinchey excused himself for another beer.

About this time the Jazz Combo took over and Hernando's Hideaway was transformed into one rhythmic, rollicking jam session. "School teaching was never like this," I thought. The harmonic pattern was there. Improvisation was there. These G.O.T. players had "it" and they were generously sharing with all other G.O.T. people—members and non-members alike.

I had just about decided to sign on the dotted line when the music stopped and the Master of Ceremonies said into the microphone for everyone to be seated—that the Union President had a message for us.

With an impressive roll of drums a tall, young man, who I later learned was Mr. Hiram Rompers, stood on the podium for attention:

"Friends," Mr. Rompers began. "Welcome to our monthly get-together. G.O.T. is glad to see so many new faces. I have only one announcement to make and it is this:

"G.O.T. has been requested to take part in the dedication of Sesqui—the satellite school over at Centennial. The date has been set—for February 1. Now you know that Sesqui is actually a portable classroom. This is a new innovation in education and Superintendent Holmes thinks it merits being dedicated. Now what would you think of our wonderful Jazz Combo playing some music for the occasion? It might blast some sense into Superintendent Holmes," Mr. Rompers added, referring to past happenings apparently which I knew nothing about. "Well, how about it?" he shouted. A ruffle of applause answered him.

"Wait a minute. Wait a minute!" came a cry from activist Jebb Hinchey. "The Jazz is terrific. We'd be honored to be represented by G.O.T's Jazz Combo. But let's be honest. Look at our men. Look at 'em. Pretty shabby, I'd say."

We looked. The tenor saxophone player had on a shaggy black turtleneck sweater. The man on the cornet was resplendent in an off-white undershirt. The clarinet man had on a seedy-looking pullover while the piano player wore an open necked flannel shirt. Jebb Hinchey spoke the truth.

"We need some class," he continued. That's what A.G.H.A.S.T. keeps accusing us of not having. Class." Then he added, knowingly: "And, I have heard rumors that the A.G.H.A.S.T. Glee Club will sing at the dedication—wearing tuxedos! Now, what say we match that? How about renting a few tuxedos for G.O.T.!" And Jebb, his duty done, slouched into the nearest chair.

"How much money have we in the treasury?" Mr. Rompers demanded.

A small, thin, bespectacled man rose to his feet, shook his head sadly and replied:

"We have only about twenty dollars—after tonight's party," he said quietly. And then he sat down, dejected.

"Tuxedos are 50 bucks apiece to rent," Mr. Rompers continued on in a sad, sad voice. "Well, it was just an idea. G.O.T. will continue to stagger along I guess, influencing no one, until we get some gold in our coffers, I suppose, and some class to our image," and he shrugged profoundly.

Whatever got into non-beer-drinking, non-card-carrying Miss Morrow I'll never know, but in the next instant I found myself raising my hand—being recognized—and ultimately saying into the microphone:

"Listen, you all, A.G.H.A.S.T. is *borrowing* some out-of-style but good-enough-looking tuxedos from the clothing collected in my room for the Tintown Clothing Drive. This is what they're using. I know. I was at their meeting. Mr. Mackin donated them from his Tuxedo Rental Business—here in Greentree. A.G.H.A.S.T. is borrowing fifty. There are twenty-six left! They're in my closet in Sesqui if you want them."

A resounding cheer—the kind that only could come from people expressing full approval at a beer party, now rose to the ceiling, pushed to the walls, and then burst out the seams of the doors in one blooming, resonant hurrah.

Mr. Rompers rattled the microphone for order—to no avail—and then left the platform to placate the Hernando Hideaway manager who, waving a towel, was demanding an explanation.

It was Jebb Hinchey, though, who got to my side first:

"You're awright, kid. Even if you never join G.O.T. you're awright."

Then it was Mr. Herendeen's turn in the din:

"Miss Morrow. The Protest Committee has just decided to give you the benefit of one of its protest marches," he shouted into my ear,—"to show our appreciation."

"What?" I shouted back, uncomprehending, "What do you mean?"

"Our Committee is organizing a picketing—to get Sesqui connected. To fix you up," he explained with the veins in his neck rising from the effort.

"But I don't want any picketing!"

I was beginning to see the picture, but my voice was swallowed up in an ocean of sound that reached the top pinnacle on an Everest of noise the same moment the Jazz Combo began an animated version of TIGER RAG.

"What a pity!" I thought disconsolately, "My teaching career is coming to an end—and it has hardly had a beginning. Shades of Mr. Birly! I could never make him understand. Never in a thousand A.G.H.A.S.T. or a million G.O.T. years!"

XVI

THE KNIGHTS FROM NEWTON'S BEANERY

The next day—Saturday—I partially convinced myself, getting out of bed at Mrs. Decklebaum's, that I had had a bad dream. When I put this thought aside, I then deemphasized incident by incident—all that had happened at the beer party, in the hope that it would all disappear into the Greentree stratosphere. When this failed to materialize I gave up and tried to plan how I would handle Mr. Birly and the promised tuxedos. I also resolved to see Mr. Herendeen the first thing Monday morning to have him call off his pickets.

And Monday morning came in one, dramatic rosy flash across the Greentree sky. At least the weather was with me, I mused as I dressed.

Walking to Sesqui, however, I detected a tintillating, tangible, tingling-tangle to the air.

"But why am I so apprehensive?" I asked myself, rounding the last corner. And there was the reason!

Spread out as plain as a red-checkered tablecloth on the grass at a family picnic was a line of pickets the length of Sesqui!

Holy Toledo! And all I would think to do was run.

As I huffed into view I could see that Mr. Herendeen was ready for me:

"Well, Miss Morrow. You see—G.O.T. keeps its word. When we say we'll picket—by damn, we picket."

"But Mr. Herendeen—who are all these men?" I protested. There must have been at least thirty.

"They're not teachers," he explained. "They're from the local cannery—Newton's Beanery—they're on the night shift. Before any of 'em went home to supper and bed they came here to do their stint," he beamed. "Now, what do you think of that?"

"But I don't understand," I continued, half-smiling back into the peering faces of at least twenty young, middle-aged and oldish men who gathered in a circle about us.

"We're from the Newton Beanery down the road. Your G.O.T. Union is an affiliation of our Union. We're all brothers together," one man offered as he radiated love for all mankind.

"When any one of our fellow unions has trouble—we come to help," said another man brandishing the sign:

SESQUI
UNCONNECTED
IS
SESQUI
<u>UNFULFILLED!</u>

—and over a stomach that was vehemently objecting to the rigidity of the sign's plywood backing.

"And," Mr. Herendeen put in, reassuringly, "when any of you need help we'd do the same for you."

"You mean that when the Newton Beanery has Labor troubles the teachers will picket for them?" I asked, unbelieving.

"Certainly," answered Mr. Herendeen. "We sent G.O.T. members up there last year—at recess time, and on their free hours. Helped a lot," he added, looking to the man on his left for his nod of approval.

"Now, men," Mr. Herendeen shouted, "disperse, disperse, for just one hour now. Just until the photographer from the News comes. Give it all you've got. Then you can go home. I'll go for coffee and doughnuts before the kids start coming and causing confusion."

"The Kids! Confusion!" It was not the children I feared but Mr. Birly who could now be seen stomping through the marigold stubble,—his coat flying,—his tie fluttering ominously. Instinctively, I got behind Mr. Herendeen who, fortunately, I thought, was bigger than Mr. Birly.

"Wha—wha—wha," Mr. Birly said, trying to get his breath and comprehend the situation all at once.

"Wha—whoa now," Mr. Herendeen corrected. Mr. Birly was his boss, too. I found this thought to be consoling.

"It's G.O.T.," Mr. Herendeen began. "G.O.T. is behind getting Sesqui connected. That's all. We're here to see that it's done."

"Wha—wha—wha," Mr. Birly stormed.

"These men," answered Mr. Herendeen, "are from the Beanery. They're free now. The teachers of course are not. They're just helping us picket."

I marveled at Mr. Herendeen's simple approach. I gloried in his absolute calm. It was as though Mr. Herendeen had said simply:

Never Pluck a Persimmon

"And good-morning to you, sir, Mr. Birly."

"Wha—wha—wha," Mr. Birly continued, looking beady-eyed at all the Sesqui signs. And then he spied a piece of me sticking out when Mr. Herendeen unexpectedly shifted his weight to the other foot.

"Miss Morrow!" he had found his tongue at last.

"Wha—wha—wha—..."

"What is the meaning of this?" I mouthed the words, my eyes closed. Then I opened them, gazing heavenward for some kind of instant help. Instant coffee, instant cream, instant help! Oh, could the heavens open?...

"Mr. Birly!..." I began hesitantly at first, but then, suddenly realizing it was no mirage, I screamed jubilantly:

"Mr. Birly! MR. BIRLY! LOOK! LOOK! IT'S THE CENTENNIAL EAGLE!

And, fortunately for me, Mr. Herendeen and the picketing beanery men—IT WAS THE CENTENNIAL EAGLE! Looping, lilting—gliding, glimmering—the Centennial Eagle! Swooping now over Sesqui.

"Men!" Mr. Birly shouted excitedly. "Help me catch that bird. The reward is $10!"

And the Sesqui signs were tossed helter-skelter onto Centennial's lawn—forgotten messages of a postponed, less-interesting, less-immediate endeavor.

"Miss Morrow," I was instructed, "go call up the Greentree Zoo to see how we might go about trapping the eagle," and I hastened to my task, relieved for the momentary distraction.

By the time the newsphotographer got on the scene to catch a glimpse and a picture of the reported pickets, the scene had changed from one of broiling, boiling politics to a serene, sublime study of Nature's own.

Indeed, by the time the Greentree Times hit the sidewalks, the picture shown of the Centennial mascot—safely now behind bars—was most gratifying. Why so many Beanery men had suddenly converged on Sesqui was never explained by the paper, and Mr. Birly, featured prominently beside the Eagle, looked pleased—with himself, and with the world about him. And that was, for my thinking, all that mattered.

Perhaps with its mascot back, an era of good luck would be in store for Sesqui-Centennial. It was something to think about, something to cross fingers over, something to spit on my palms about. By all the toads, toadstools, pollywogs and warts in existence, maybe there would yet be a future for both Sesqui and myself.

XVII

THE MONEY DRIVE

But, double, double, toil and trouble; fire burn and caldron bubble! I had been worrying so much about how to approach Mr. Birly concerning giving G.O.T. the tuxedos that I had forgotten about Mr. Jackson's fervent dedication to a connected-Sesqui. The Privy Counselor had, in the intervening weeks, organized, and Greentree, therefore, hadn't a chance. The Money Drive was on! Every child, every adult, every citizen was important to Mr. Jackson. Here was a potential contributor to THE FUND! And no one escaped. "Save the trees AND Sesqui!" the signs all read.

He had set up collection cans beside every cash register in every store, along with a sad, sad picture of Sesqui. With Mrs. Jackson he organized fashion shows, dog shows, rummage sales and bake sales. Enterprise was the watchword,—a connected Sesqui the goal of all 'interested' individuals. The only obstacle came from the fact that the entire citizenry had not the fanatic enthusiasm for the project that the Jacksons had.

True, there were those who wanted Sesqui connected. But there were also those who did not. There were those on the School Board who favored raising money for THE CAUSE. There were still the members of the Opposition who considered it a waste of time and energy and possibly, bladder-fortitude. And of course there was G.O.T. who put body and soul behind Sesqui and A.G.H.A.S.T. who persisted in dragging her feet at "the very idea of a Sesqui with plumbing!"

Even the inhabitants of Sesqui itself—those most intimately involved—were hopelessly divided. There were those with the weak kidneys and those with the iron ones. The weak ones contributed their pennies with desperate, frenzied gusto, while the others gave reluctantly and only when some particular project especially appealed to them.

The chocolate pudding party—open only to Sesqui-ites—netted a chocolate-spotted, lemony-beige rug and $1.55. Sandy, our nature-lover, suggested we grow something and so, cucumber seeds were planted in long narrow boxes and placed along the windows. When the seedlings were ready and the danger from frost over, they would be placed on top of Sesqui's roof and eventually, we hoped, sold on the open market as pickles, or cucumbers, or what-have-you. But neither the Sesqui-ites nor

Never Pluck a Persimmon

the cucumbers arrived at this point. The seeds sprouted beautifully, too beautifully, in fact, and so they were placed on the roof to soak up the Indiana sun and warm spring rains. But when vine after vine crept over and down and around, and above and beyond and in and out, covering the Sesqui windows one by one, in a glorious proclamation to glorious Spring, Mr. Birly ordered the defoliation of Sesqui, and so we stood naked and penniless from this thwarted endeavor.

But, actually, Sesqui's main contribution to the Money Drive was the producing and selling of modernistic pictures which were titled "Life As We See It—from Sesqui." For some reason the Greentree citizens who were <u>FOR</u> having us connected wanted a little something from the <u>Source,</u> and they opened their pocketbooks willingly. They clamored for the pictures which were eventually exhibited at every dog show for $1.00 apiece. When the demand exceeded the supply we abandoned our paint brushes and embraced mechanized mass production. Each Monday after school—since this was the only time the club-meeting room over in Centennial was available—Henry Burnett, under my direction, would cautiously spread out newspapers over the huge floor in preparation for <u>The Painting</u>. Then, Robert Jackson followed, placing manila paper side by side atop the newspapers. Mary Jane came last, dropping plops of multi-colored paints haphazardly over the papers. Then, at the sound of my whistle, Robert, Mary Jane, and Henry would mount their bicycles and would ride through and around and in and up and down and over and out—through the paint. When the tire designs were "expressive" enough I would then signal with the whistle to stop. The cleaning of the bikes took more time than the picture-painting. One hundred-two versions of "Life as We See It from Sesqui" were sold, netting $102—give or take a dollar—for The Fund. Not a meager contribution by any means! $102 could buy some copper tubing—or some pipe fittings—or maybe the chrome fixtures for a Sesqui sink. And, when an honest-to-God plumber actually came with tape measurement and a notebook and pencil and wrote things down and made some curlicue calculations, well...we all began to see that a connected Sesqui might very well become a reality and something gone from our imaginations—forever!

The fact that the School Board had still not given official permission did not deter Mr. Jackson nor his committee. There was the general belief—prevalent in the entire community—that if the money materialized, so, also would the toilets. And, because John Calhoun Jones was president of the Board and he favored Sesqui being connected, well...

But a Sesqui-Supporter whom no one had anticipated was Miss Forester, Art Supervisor and steadfast A.G.H.A.S.T.inian, as well as the persimmon recipe-burner. Miss Forester's vivid imagination seemed to be fired by Sesqui's plight. It was possible, too, that she had felt somewhat responsible since the hex signs the third-graders had drawn were done in the name of 'Art'. Would she reverse the bad-luck trend?

It was Miss Forester, therefore, who sponsored the Creative Cookery Contest in the town and who eventually made a minor mint merely by manipulating Greentree cooks one against the other.

To enter the contest a cook had, first of all, to pay the entry fee—$2.00 per entry. But Miss Forester, shrewd-like, would not accept the entire $2.00, but insisted on turning fifty cents of each entry back to the grocer where the housewife bought her ingredients. In this way the contestant represented herself and the corner grocer and the Grocer, therefore, tried to get all his customers to participate in the contest since it was profitable for him, too. This swelled the number of contestants considerably.

As far as the business side went Miss Forester had no equal but the culinary side of it all had townspeople talking to themselves. There was a designated "Space Category" an "Equatorial Category" (recipes specializing in tropical fruits were wanted here)—an "Old World" category, a "Pennsylvania Dutch Dish," an "Oriental" department, delights from the "Dark Continent" and an "Operation Understanding."

The fact that no entry ever materialized for Operation Understanding gave the local ministers and social workers cause for concern but any Greentree cook worth her salt knew instinctively that this pitfall was not for her.

Not content with the adult end of the contest, however, Miss Forester stretched her imagination even farther and came up with a Head-Start cookery division which had the walls of Greentree kitchens smeared with peanut butter and mango jelly and which netted a nebulous assortment of nettled parents-—but no contest entries.

Because of Mr. Birly's affiliation with Sesqui, though, Miss Forester thought it fitting and proper to appoint him official taster and judge of all entries. I could therefore imagine Miss Forester in my mind's eye "directing" Mr. Birly's efforts as she had directed Sesqui's third graders with their paper sculptures.

Never Pluck a Persimmon

"Now—take a taste!

"Twist it 'round!

"Smack your lips together!" I could hear her saying. And I could see the avant-garde eyes rolling with the pitch.

But the actual judging took place in the privacy of the Centennial P.T.A. kitchen so the general public—along with myself—was denied the experience of witnessing the event. The Greentree Times, however, went into great detail proclaiming the victorious cooks and complimenting all the winners. The winners, they said, did Mr. Birly proud.

In the "Space Category," FLYING SAUCER MARBLE CAKE" flew to the very top, as did "TAHITI TREASURE" in the tropical division. This winner utilized even coconut tree bark in some unexplained way. "FANCY YET PLAIN", a pumpernickel of a sort with more than a nickel's worth of flavor, took the honors for the "Pennsylvania Dutch," and Mrs. Jackson herself won the "Dark Continent" category with "A KNIGHT TO REMEMBER"—a chocolate ladyfinger with a neuter-almond filling. What the News failed to report, however, and which I learned weeks afterwards, was that all the food remaining from the contest was taken as usual to the Greentree Day Care for the children to enjoy. Possibly because the kids just weren't used to Creative Cookery and/or possibly because they were used to more palatable fare—the fact remains that when the "CELERY SOUP BREAD" entry was served at one table the kids positively revolted. They threw their glasses of milk into the nearby brick fireplace while others who were exposed to "GRAPEFRUIT UPSIDE DOWN CAKE" did likewise.

Financially speaking, however, the Creative Cookery Contest was extremely successful. The money collected from this and from all endeavors would be presented to Superintendent Holmes at Sesqui's Dedication. It was to be the high point of the evening.

As February 1st approached, the preparations were gaining momentum. The A.G.H.A.S.T. Glee Club rehearsed on the Centennial stage every other day—or so it seemed. Mr. Birly had already picked up the tuxedos he needed from my closet—so A.G.H.A.S.T. was all set. But I still had G.O.T.'s in tow. How, oh how could I break the news to Mr. Birly that I had taken it upon myself to authorize their wearing them? When he hated G.O.T.'s guts? When I was the teacher lowest on the Sesqui-Centennial totem pole?

In the meantime another wire from Tintown arrived:

"TUXEDOS HAVE NOT YET ARRIVED STOP PLEASE ADVISE."

"We'll send them February 2," Mr. Birly told me. "I've extended the Clothing Drive to then."

Oh! How I wished the Dedication would come and get everything over with...Then I could relax—and Tintown could get the tuxedos—and Mr. Birly...

"I don't understand this arithmetic problem," Mary Jane brought me to earth again. "Would you please go over it again?"

"Miss Morrow," interrupted Henry. "Clifford is chewing gum."

"I am not," Clifford was indignant.

"You are so," Henry shot back.

"Boys...boys," I aimed for peace.

And then Clifford changed the subject:

"Miss Morrow," he said, putting his hands on his hips, "My Mother wants to know. What did you do with her gallstones? She wants them back. And, she's tired waiting."

I bit my lip. Whereas Clifford used to request his Mother's gallstones once a week it was now a daily happening.

"Clifford," I said quietly. "I have told you many times. I do not have your Mother's gallstones. The Science Fair Committee never returned them. But," I added, "I will write another note to your Mother explaining this again," and I turned back to my desk, a limp dish cloth from which every single drop of greasy dishwater had been wrung.

I was a plucked chicken without so much as a whisper of a hair of a feather left! I was a glob of pancake batter spread out on a flat, flat griddle. But because I had no baking powder ingredient I was doomed never to rise, never to rise, never to rise...

Why wouldn't this woman respond to reason? She had an obsession...and to forget, I began to help Mary Jane with her arithmetic. "When you are finished with your problems, class," I struggled for strength to speak, "you may read a library book at the reading table."

Then, glancing over at the collection of books I spotted a favorite Dr. Seuss.

Dr. Seuss was a man who could write Clifford's Mother a note she'd never forget. She might even come to understand...

So inspired, I began:

Never Pluck a Persimmon

Dear Mrs. Richards:

Your gallstones are not here nor there.
Your gallstones are not anywhere.
We looked to find them in a hat.
We thought they might be in our cat.

And then we found this one ol' jar.
"Jar!" we said. "What have we ar'?"
Slimy traces on the glass!
Had this housed a slimy mass?"

Because the cat ate one canary
(at Science Fair)—it makes us wary...
Empty jar plus stoney stare!
"Cat!" I said, "what ails you there?"
"Sticks and stones will break your bones!
"But it's stones—just stones!" the ol' cat moans.

Therefore:
Your gallstones are not here nor there.
Your gallstones are not anywhere.
You will not find them in a house.
You will not find them in a mouse.
So, prithee, be content with Sesqui,
And cease your being so darn pesqui!

P.S. You will not find them in a hat.
But you just might find them in our cat.

It was with great satisfaction, then, that I signed the note and gave it to Clifford for his Mother.

And one week later a curt note, with package attached, came for me—from Centennial, from Mr. Birly, from the Principal's Office.

"Miss Morrow," it stated starkly, "True. We cannot find Clifford's Mother's gallstones but we must find a more diplomatic way of stating this simple truth than by explaining our position via sarcastic poetry. Attached find examples of notes I have been collecting through the years that show the shining quality you must strive to attain if you are to become a successful teacher."

So-o-o-o-o.

And there they were—neatly stacked gems of diplomacy—to Mother after Mother—about her most precious possessions:

Dear Mother,

Your son Johnny's aim at the latrine is extremely poor. There have been complaints. Would you please practice with him in his (and your) free time?

Understandingly,

Dear Mother,

It was clever of you, and very generous, to provide the class with your home-made fortune cookies for our Bunny-Hop party.

In the future, however, would you please refrain from such predictions as—"You will make an 'A' in your next English test"—as it creates complex problems for both teacher and pupil alike. Thank you.

Sincerely,

Dear Mother,

I am sorry you misunderstood but your Ernest is not a *patrol* boy but a *parole* boy. This means he must report to the principal at the beginning of each day to tell him of his behavior and whereabouts the night before.

This will explain why he has not been issued the patrol badge and belt.

Sincerely,

Dear Mother,

Jerome tells me he was born in the back seat of an automobile. Could you please tell me which city and which state you were in at the time—so that I may get my records up to date?

Sincerely,

Dear Mother,

I am sorry but Mary Jo has earned an "F" in creative clayness. She has made nothing but worms this entire semester, and I personally feel that worms and snakes lack creative spontaneity. Perhaps you might suggest something in the Crustacean family for next semester. This would perhaps give her the opportunity of making claws, etc. which would entail more details, and hence, more creativity.

Sincerely,

Dear Mother,

I do believe it is time for Robbie to have an allowance of his own. This may possibly deter him from looking for small change in my purse when my back is turned.

Sincerely,

Dear Mother,

This noon Sara Sue did not eat her strawberry whipped gelatine, her vegetarian vegetable thermos of soup, nor the carrot curls and celery sticks which you so painstakingly packed in her lunch. She did take one bite from the nectarine, however, and consumed one half of the one-half pint carton of milk.

If I may be presumptuous, my suggestion for tomorrow's lunch is as follows: Throw two slices of baloney onto two slices of bread. Put on no mayonnaise, no butter, no lettuce, no tomato. Do not cut sandwich in half. Roll sandwich in globs of crookedly-cut waxed paper. Include no napkin. Throw sandwich into paper sack.

I predict:

The casual approach to eating will result in the improvement of Sara Sue's appetite. I can verify this from my years of teaching. The robust, healthy children carry the fruitless, vegetable-less, baloney-ladened lunches whereas the thin, scrawny children are those who always seem to be inundated with thermos-equipped lunch boxes complete with dry-ice compartments with toothpaste and toothbrushes enclosed.

Sincerely

Dear Mother,

Each time I stop at Arthur's desk he blows his nose in a fashion that sounds like the Bronx Cheer. This could be coincidence and I realize I could be overly-suspicious. But will you please speak to him about this?

Sincerely,

Dear Mother,
Your son James has the mistaken notion that "but" is not a conjunction. It is also, according to his idea, *not* the remains of a cigarette or cigar. Would you please have a little talk with him?

Sincerely,

Dear Mother,
It is nice that Charlotte has panties marked for every day of the week but it is a drawback to the discipline of my room.

When I ask if anyone can tell me the day of the week, Charlotte promptly lifts her dress and consults her panties and yells out the answer. When a spelling word is a day of the week, Charlotte again consults her panties. It is getting so now that instead of consulting me, the teacher, the children look first to Charlotte and her weekly series of panties.

Would you please settle for plain pink or white—without any information whatsoever on them—in the future? Thank you.

Sincerely,

Dear Mother,
Karen of late has a baffling habit of placing her head upside down on the floor—while still remaining in her seat—and looking at me from this angle. When questioned she says: "But you look prettier this way."

I suggest you send her to an eye doctor—just to be sure. In the meantime, I have signed up for an Accelerated Beauty Course to see what can be done.

Sincerely,

Dear Mother,
Our pet parakeet escaped from the cage the janitor had made for it during "Farmer in the Dell" time this a.m. The bird

apparently was trying to make a break for it because it flew immediately to the window, apparently heading for the great outdoors, but was thwarted by the glass—thwarted to such an extent, in fact, that it crashed and fell stunned to the floor.

Your little Ellen, intent on singing "the child takes a nurse" did not see the bird and backed up. The bird, unfortunately, was as flat as a pancake.

This, however, explains Ellen's tear-stained face as well as what she has in the box with the pink ribbon on it. She insisted on a formal burial.

Sincerely,

Dear Mother,

I would suggest you wash out Jeremy's mouth sometime this evening. Three times this afternoon the Red Cross Life Saver Swimmer jumped into the Centennial pool thinking he was calling "Help!" to fish Jeremy out. And, three times, Jeremy was not saying "Help!" but was merely expressing frustration at not being able to execute the backstroke effectively.

Sincerely,

P.S. Something with hexachlorophine in it might prove more lasting.

Dear Mother,

I wouldn't worry about the results of the Kuner Interest Test. The fact that Jamie came out under "Shepherd" is no reason to believe that he will not be gainfully employed in his future when an adult.

Sincerely,

Dear Mother,

The lunches in the cafeteria are extremely nutritious and delightfully edible. The fact that Junior merely mistook the chocolate sauce for gravy and put this into a well-defined moat in his mashed potatoes is no reason to denounce the entire Centennial lunch program. I would suggest you serve a lighter colored gravy at home in the future to provide him with guidance in selecting his culinary fare.

Sincerely,

"Yes," I thought to myself as I read the last of the notes, "I see what Mr. Birly means. Diplomacy. Say what you mean but be diplomatic about it."

I had much to learn. But what was encouraging was the fact that I could see that all teachers had problems. No one had an easy time of it. As I walked back to Centennial to return Mr. Birly's treasured collection, I mulled these things over and vowed to try to do better.

I had gone only a short distance when I spied Sandy who was on her way to the playground down the street.

"Hi," I waved.

Sandy waved back and then back-tracked a bit and ran toward me.

"Miss Morrow," she panted, approaching, "I've been thinking about you all day."

"Oh?" I couldn't imagine what was coming.

"Yes," Sandy went on, "And I think that—really and truly—you're the poorest teacher I ever had."

The words were spoken. They had pierced my insides like a butter knife slicing Jello.

"Why, Sandy!" I gasped, amazed at the child's perception. This child felt my inadequacies. Or, she could see right through them. Yet, the poorest of, say, four teachers. Sandy would have had a Kindergarten Teacher, First Grade, Second...thank God, I was not a Senior High School Teacher and have this said to me...

"Yes," Sandy was continuing. "You have no color t.v. and no car—you're really the poorest teacher I have ever had!"

Sandy. Dear Sandy. I smiled to myself. Why, I had no problems. As long as I had one dear little Sandy around...I could bear anything.

I could bear a Sesqui—forever unconnected! I could take A.G.H.A.S.T. and G.O.T. one at a time—or together. I could tolerate Mr. Birly...

"Have a good time at the play-ground," I said to the little upturned face. "And don't worry about a colored t.v., Mrs. Decklebaum has one. And I'm going to make a down payment on a car next month."

"Oh, good!" Sandy answered, relieved and reassured. "I'm so glad!" And we parted ways.

Yes, I told myself. God was in His heaven. All's right with the world. As long as I had a Sandy, all <u>was</u> right...well, almost all right.

And I went in to see my Principal, Mr. Birly, from Centennial School, Greentree, Indiana—to thank him for his help.

XVIII

Extra-Curricular Activities

"Miss Morrow," Mr. Birly greeted me, looking up from his desk. "You're just the person I want to see," he began.

And before one minute had expired I found myself nominated, elected and inaugurated Chairman of the Refreshment Committee for the Dedication of Sesqui.

"But I've never done anything like this before," I protested.

"Oh," Mr. Birly replied, "It just means getting a few cookies and some punch together. It's nothing to worry about."

"Do you suppose cookies and punch will be enough?" I queried timidly.

"Indubitably," Mr. Birly said, going back to his work.

"And," he added, shaking his finger, "Buy the cookies soon so we're sure to have them. They stay fresh." Then, going back to his papers he directed:

"Mr. Toothaker, the Treasurer of the P.T.A., will give you the money you need." And I was dismissed.

But what the P.T.A. Treasurer gave me was one bag of peanuts when I needed to buy a ton of them!

"Five dollars!" I screamed into the mouthpiece of the phone. "For all those people you're going to give me five dollars?!"

"Look," the Man-Treasurer was saying into my ear, "We're trying to squeeze every penny we can—for Sesqui—for you. We want a big sum—we want to make a big splash when we present the grand total to Superintendent Holmes. But," he added indulgently, "we can let you have $5.00."

"Five dollars for all those cookies and all the punch I'll need—for a couple of hundred people is ridiculous!" I reiterated my stand. Even though I had never been a Chairman of any Refreshment Committee before, I knew I was not up to any Loaves and Fishes approach.

"Tell you what," Mr. Toothaker advised. "You go over to Charley's Supermarket on the east side. He's got bargains. Real bargains. No kidding. You'll get a break from Charley. I'll bet you any money that the five spot will do it over at his Supermarket."

I couldn't fight City Hall. I couldn't even fight the Treasurer of the P.T.A. What was the use?

"Okay," I said. "Send me the five. I'll see what I can do."

So it was a few days later that I approached Charley's Supermarket on a roundabout way home after school. And, it was true. Charley had the goods.

Charley had all kinds of bargains. And he did have packaged cookies in a variety of kinds.

"Perhaps I could ice them," I thought to myself. "If I took them from their wrappings—frosted them in say, different colors, why perhaps they would never be recognized as the cheapest of the cheap..."

"Have a nice party," Charley said as he rang up $4.98 on his register.

Walking home I concluded that the "project" would not be too involved. Mrs. Decklebaum would help me, I was sure. She was a very willing woman. Since her children were grown and married she did have time on her hands.

And so it was that the two of us proceeded to unpack the cookies an evening or so later and commenced to "doctor" them up. We had whipped up some chocolate fudge frosting, some banana creme filling and some nougat nicety.

"The Skin-flint!" Mrs.Decklebaum said, referring to Mr. Toothaker, looking over the cookies. "He must think we're magicians!"

"He wouldn't care if we served mud pies," I said, "as long as it would keep money in his old P.T.A. account. But think what it would do to my reputation as Chairman of the Refreshment Comm..."

The word was never completed.

"MRS. DECKLEBAUM!" I gasped. "LOOK!"

"Look at these cookies," I hissed. "At the bottoms. Every last one has a bite taken out of it!"

"NO. It couldn't be true!" Mrs. Decklebaum commented, her eyes wide as family-sized pizzas. She peered suspiciously into the bag.

One by one we extricated them. It was so. Every last cookie had an uneven hole in center bottom, with corresponding teeth-marks in evidence.

"These are not mice teeth," I Sherlocked. "They're much too large. They look like human teeth to me!"

"Surely to God, no!" Mrs. Decklebaum protested.

One after one of the little cakes was examined. By the time we had reached the last dozen we were indeed convinced that I should make a flying trip back to the market. At least half had been tampered with.

"No wonder Charley is so cheap," I commented sourly. "He can afford to be."

"But dearie," put in Mrs. Decklebaum, "why don't you take them and show them to your Principal. Maybe he'd even give you a ride to Charley's. It's a good distance. I hate to see you lugging all these back there again and walkin' home in the dark. Why not wait 'til tomorrow?" Mrs. Decklebaum had a point. Besides, Mr. Birly should know about Charley. And Mr. Toothaker should know, too...I decided to wait until tomorrow. The holes in all the cookies would still be there, and Mr. Birly's avant-garde eyes would see the evidence, firsthand.

And the next afternoon, when I had concluded my demonstration of the mauled-over cookies, I put the question to him:

"Well, Mr. Birly," I said in conclusion, "what do you think?"

"I think we'd best head for Charley's Supermarket," he answered, reaching for his hat.

Driving through Greentree with an honest-to-God Principal at my elbow was something I never thought I would ever experience. The bag containing the cookies was balanced on my lap.

"We'll get to the bottom of this," Mr. Birly promised, manipulating his Edsel, or whatever. I searched the dashboard for information about the make of car so that I would have something to talk about but could find nothing.

It was imperative therefore that we kept returning to the half-eaten cookies.

"What do you think Charley will do, Mr. Birly?" I prompted.

"He'd better do something positive about passing off his garbage on the unsuspecting public," he said wryly, shifting the floor stick again.

Mr. Birly then swung brusquely into the cindered parking lot alongside of Charley's. Together, then, we entered the market through the Electric-Eye door.

Fortunately, Charley was not busy.

I quickly explained my errand, dumping some of the cookies out on the nearest counter for his perusal. Mr. Birly stood by my side, a sour look on his face—a look anyone could interpret as one seeking justice.

In a tired kind of way Charley picked up one after the other of the cookies.

Finally, he spoke:

"Lady," he said "and Gentleman," he added, including Mr. Birly, "use your head. Heads," he corrected. Charley seemed close to tears.

"Why would anyone—any human, let's say—take a little bite like this out of every single cookie? To begin with,...he'd have one hell of a time getting at the middles. He'd have to have 'beaver teeth'.

"Why wouldn't whoever you're accusing just <u>eat</u> a couple of dozen? Why bother nibbling this way—and in such difficult spots?" His eyes were filled with pathos—FOR <u>ME</u> <u>AND</u> MR. BIRLY! I looked to my Principal for guidance.

"Well...I never thought..." Mr. Birly was saying—

"Lady," Charley continued, "and Gentleman," he said to Mr. Birly, "these marks were made when the baker took the cookies off the cookie sheets. See...part of the cookie...the middle...stuck...stayed on the sheet—that's why you've got holes, lady, holes in the middle of every cookie!" He was truly exasperated.

"As for the teeth marks," he went on, "whatever instrument—or knife—was used to remove the cookies from the sheets—these—and these alone, lady,—and Gentleman," he included Mr. Birly, "made what you say are 'teethmarks'!"

"But," Charley still wasn't finished, "tell you what I'll do. I'll give you cookies—with all the middles in. I want you to be satisfied. And," he added with finality, "I'll go over every single package myself!" and he was off, to make good his word.

Never Pluck a Persimmon

Instead of turning immediately to face Mr. Birly I decided to scrutinize the scallions that were conveniently located straight ahead—in neatly arranged rows, near other neatly-arranged rows of robust-looking radishes.

"Miss Morrow," Mr. Birly was stating a fact again. "The next time I appoint you Chairman of a Refreshment Committee—will you remind me that you have served your term?" His words stabbed me like an ice pick cutting hot water.

"Yes sir," I answered, still contemplating the scallions and concluding that at 95¢ a sack—and unscathed by human teeth—they were indeed a bargain—a bargain which might indeed interest the public-minded, principled, populace of Greentree, Indiana.

XIX

THE PEEPING TOM

"Miss Morrow," Mr. Birly whispered mysteriously to me as I picked up my mail in Centennial the next morning, "I have a favor to ask of you." And I was subsequently ushered into Mr. Birly's immaculate wood-paneled office, and the door was closed.

"Wh...wh...wh...?" I felt like asking, but I couldn't get it out.

"It was brought to my attention," he began slowly enough, "last evening by one of our parents," he added, "that," he was certainly taking his time, "our Centennial lavatory has a Peeping Tom!"

With this his voice took on a profound kind of horror!

"No!" I gasped, thankful that deprived Sesqui hadn't this nasty problem.

"Wh...wh...wh...What can we do about it?" I asked, still stunned.

Mr. Birly's eyebrows were arched now, like a jungle cat about to spring.

"You can do a lot," Mr. Birly said, "if you will."

"Of course," I agreed, "anything!"

"Well," said Mr. Birly, "I have asked Mrs. Puternaugh to come today to take over your class."

"What!" I was astounded. "But I'm here!" I was indignant. A substitute when I'm here! Whatever could he be thinking about?

"I want you to do some spying for me!" Mr. Birly said matter-of-factly.

"I'm a schoolteacher, not Mata Hari," I thought wildly.

Instead I voiced:

"What did you have in mind, Mr. Birly?"

"I'd like for you to station yourself in the girl's lavatory—all day long—to catch this culprit!" Mr. Birly declared emphatically.

"All day?" I was aghast.

"All day," Mr. Birly repeated, "and keep your eyes open," he added.

I knew they would be.

"I'd do it myself," Mr. Birly continued, stating a fact, "but...but...well, I can't." Mr. Birly was aware of his limitations.

"But a whole day..." I started to say.

Never Pluck a Persimmon

"We must apprehend this villain," Mr. Birly's eyes were on their way up again.

"Now," he continued with the plan, "I've asked Mr. Hubbard the custodian to station himself on the roof—behind the chimney—to stand watch from there," he kept outlining.

"On the roof?" I repeated. This was indeed a conspiracy.

"Well, the Peeping Tom was seen at the window in there—and there's only the one window—and," he added, calculatingly, "he could reach that window from the roof, so-o-o."

"Yes," I followed him, waiting for more.

"Well, with you stationed inside, and Mr. Hubbard outside—we can't lose," Mr. Birly was pleased with his plan.

"But it's cold out," I protested on behalf of Mr. Hubbard.

"Mr. Hubbard has thermal underwear," he assured me. "He's also bringing a thermos of hot coffee."

"Mr. Birly," I had to clear a few things up in my mind. "Who was it who saw this...this Peeping Tom? Are they sure?"

"Little Suzette Thompson, a Kindergartener, saw him," Mr. Birly answered. "I spoke to her mother and her father. She's quite upset."

"But..." I hesitated somewhat, "couldn't one that young be...be mistaken?"

"No," Mr. Birly said confidentially, "I questioned her myself." And here he cleared his throat: "Suzette said that a boy was looking in through that window at her and she pointed to the window to show me."

Well, there was nothing more to be said...

"But, Mr. Birly," I had to ask it, "what can I possibly do in there all day long?"

"You would be doing the school a tremendous service with your sacrifice," Mr. Birly showed his teeth, and I was dismissed.

"And, Miss Morrow," Mr. Birly added as I was about to go through his door, "remember...we're keeping what you're doing a secret—in order to catch..."

"I understand," I assured him, wondering how in the name of heaven I could appear invisible all day in the girl's john...

...If I were a cocoon I could be enwrapped in tissue paper. But, perhaps I could hide in the tall paper basket...or crouch in a stall...with my feet tucked up...or perhaps I could hang myself on the coat hook on the door, if there was a coat hook on the door, holding my feet up the while...

And how Mrs. Puternaugh welcomed her assignment!

"Thank you for all the...improvements," I told her as I retrieved a box of tissues from my desk in preparation for my spying mission.

"Oh, I enjoy fixing things up!" Mrs. Puternaugh was being polite.

"That pulley was especially clever," I told her, "and I really appreciate it." I was now edging my way to the door. I did not want Mrs. Puternaugh asking me questions about my "secret" mission.

"The plans are on the desk," I kept talking, "and..."

"Never fear. Never fear," Mrs. Puternaugh assured me. "When the children get here all will be in readiness," she smiled warmly now. One was sorely tempted to chuck her under her chin.

"Fine," I replied, waving now from the doorway.

I almost made it.

"But what kind of 'special' work will you be doing today?" she put it to me. There, Mrs. Puternaugh had got to it!

"Intelligence work," I answered winking knowingly.

Mrs. Puternaugh winked back and waved me on my way.

At the door of Centennial's Girls' Lavatory I was met by Mr. Hubbard who already had everything under control.

"Here," he said, shoving a can of Fragrant-Air into my hand. "Would you like some coffee?"

"Later," I replied.

"Well," he shrugged resignedly, "I guess we'd better get to our posts before anyone comes in."

"Before the children get here," I restated his sentence. "Yes." I agreed.

"Lissen. I put a chair in there for you—facing the window," he said.

"Fine," I replied, "and thank you."

And then we parted, I, around the corner into the pink-polished tiled, six-stalled, well-mirrored girls' restroom, and Mr. Hubbard to his precariously-situated, purposefully-perched position on the roof. And the day began.

During the first hour I discovered that the pink tiles numbered 1,632 on the north wall and 1,492 on the south wall—give or take a few for the paper towel container.

During the second hour I found the Centennial's fine quality of tissue paper could be twisted into ethereal-looking, delicate carnations—give a tear here and a twist there.

By the third hour I knew the job could be profitable when a seventh grader thrust a dime into my hand on her way out.

During the third hour also I was relieved for a half hour—by Mr. Birly's secretary, Mrs. Strong.

"I'll take over for fifteen minutes now," she said. "Hurry and get some relaxation."

"Thank you," I replied, turning my plastic lawn chair over to her for safe-keeping.

In the hall, however, I was very surprised to meet Mr. Hubbard.

"But I thought you were on the roof," I greeted him.

"I was," he replied, "but Mr. Birly's up there now—I'm supposed to get warmed up."

"The changing of the guard—right here in Greentree," I said to myself, nodding again to Mr. Hubbard who looked as though he might permanently have to hold his arms now at those awful angles.

"Pretty cold up there, I guess," I commented to make conversation.

"It's damn cold up there," he corrected and left to find a radiator.

Fortunately, for me, but unfortunately for Mr. Birly and Mrs. Strong, Suzette Thompson's bathroom-time coincided with my coffee break and Mr. Hubbard's thawing-out period.

It happened while Suzette was washing her hands—her eyes intent on the window—and Mrs. Strong's eyes right with hers, of course,—that Suzette suddenly dropped the soap, pointed a wet finger to the window, and screamed:

"THE BOY! THE BOY!"

At this, Mrs. Strong, seeing nothing, pushed the lawn chair over to the window to get a better look and to also thump a warning to Mr. Birly.

And, if it hadn't been recess time perhaps it would have all come out much better than it did. But when Mr. Birly heard the pounding on the window he left his position behind the chimney and ran to see what Mrs. Strong wanted, and then all the kids on the playground got a good look.

"It's Mr. Birly! It's Mr. Birly!" they clamored and cheered from the yard.

And they jumped up and down at the sight of their principal creeping stealthily around on the roof like Jack the Ripper or somesuch...

And all this would have passed in a few moments but for the fact that a vigilant neighbor who did not understand what was going on, called the police about a prowler in stark sunlight trapped on Centennial's roof...

It was a cruising deputy, a newcomer to Greentree, who arrived on the scene then and straightened everything out, but not before administering the sobriety test to Mr. Birly.

But Mrs. Strong, in the meantime, was making tremendous strides in the Girls' Lavatory. In getting down from the chair, she inadvertently stepped on the cake of soap that Suzette had thrown on the floor when she spotted the boy. By the time Suzette assisted Mrs. Strong to her feet, they had become good friends, worthy of confidence.

"What did the boy look like?" Mrs. Strong asked her, hoping Mr. Birly had nabbed him by this time out on the roof.

"M-m-m-m," Suzette smiled, "pretty."

But then her eyes darkened and she frowned. Tucking her little hands beneath her armpits she gazed with wide wonder into the depths of Mrs. Strong's green-grey eyes. And then, flapping her arms down and up, then up and down, she fearfully confided:

"Dat boy say 'whoo-oo-oo-oo!'"

"That boy?" Mrs. Strong was still glassy-eyed from her fall.

"Dat BOYD," Suzette corrected, and flapped her wings again to make her point.

And while the deputy finished up with Mr. Birly and I finished my coffee, and Mr. Hubbard finished his warming up, the white owl, a pet of the entire neighborhood's, went dutifully about the task of getting its food.

And the case of the Peeping Tom was forever closed.

At Centennial School.

In the small community of Greentree, Indiana.

Population 12,000, and one white owl.

XX

THE FIELD TRIP

There was yet another project that had to be endured at Sesqui-Centennial every school year. It was that of the Class Trip.

"Is our field trip before or after the Dedication?" Robert Jackson asked one morning from his seat in the reading circle.

"It's two days before the Dedication—now where were we?" I answered, getting back to "The Story of the Post Office."

"Are we going to see a field?" asked Henry Burnett, his forehead all wrinkled.

"No," I answered. "We see fields every day. We're just going to visit places you may not have been before right here in Greentree. We'll go to the Police Station, the Fire Station, and the Train Station."

"Not the Post Office?" Sandy asked, thinking about the lesson for the day.

"No," I answered.

"I've seen the Police Station!" put in Leon, "when my Dad was there."

"Why was he there?" piped up Mary Jane, her eyes wide with curiosity.

"He pulled a knife on someone," Leon answered before I could stop him.

"Boys and girls, now, please,...let's get back to the lesson," I protested. But it was Unita now who took us off the track again.

"Miss Morrow," she began, raising her hand and smiling in her winsome way, "my birthday's comin' and my Momma is lettin' me bring cup cakes and ice cream for the party." And she sat back, pleased.

This news was received with great enthusiasm by the reading circle. Then, from the reading circle it spread to those working arithmetic problems at their desks. It was as though a stone had been cast into the stream of water and the immediate circle that formed about the stone gave way to a larger circle until, eventually, it spread to the whole river.

"A Birthday Party!" Robert Jackson rubbed his stomach. "M-m-m-m~m-m-m."

But Clifford was not pleased.

"Miss Morrow," he began. "Unita's mother better not bring in chocolate ice cream because I get sick on chocolate ice cream and..."

"We'll get back to the lesson," I remonstrated for the last time, and then remembered that we had not settled all the problems for the class trip. I therefore decided to take advantage of the general confusion to add yet another distraction:

"By the way," I said, "we'll need five mothers—with cars—for the Class Trip. If any of your mothers can come next Tuesday tell them to sign the slip of paper you'll take home today."

And this time we really did get back to the reading lesson.

By the time Tuesday had come five mothers had signed on the dotted line—Mrs. Jackson, Mrs. Mackin, Mrs. Burnett, Mary Jane's mother—Mrs. Williamson, and Clifford's mother—Mrs. Richards, the woman whose gallstones I had already become acquainted with.

They came, with their horns honking and their hankies waving. And the kids piled in.

"I brought a suitcase full of sandwiches for munchies," Mrs. Mackin clucked, "Something for everyone to nibble on!"

"Fine!" I smiled back, checking the cars now with my alphabetical list.

"There better not be anything chocolate," put in Clifford's mother.

"My Clifford can't have chocolate. It upsets him." She made sure Mrs. Mackin heard her.

"No chocolate," Mrs. Mackin reassured.

And we pushed the buttons down on all the car doors.

We were off!

A few streets here, one or two red-lights, and we were at the Greentree Municipal Police Station. It was with delirious gusto that the third-graders invaded this stronghold of justice. Here they were permitted to minutely examine each on-duty Policeman's badge, unlock and lock the cell doors, provided they were vacant, and to sit, one at a time, at the Sergeant's desk to "get the feel of things." Henry Burnett, however, was the only one who mastered the dubious art of getting a spit in the center of the brass spittoon.

But at the Fire Station, things did not work out as well. The beautiful Dalmatian, in her eager attempt to welcome the Sesqui-ites, inadvertently knocked Mary Jane to the ground. This, then, resulted in at least half a dozen electing to remain in the cars. This cut confusion considerably at the

Never Pluck a Persimmon

Fire Station, but it did allow for more energy to be spent at the Train Station.

It was therefore at the Train Station that the Class Trip took on the aspect of a flea circus addicted to crack!

There were licorice drops to be purchased at the Terminal Counter. There were toilets to be tried—flushed and reflushed. There were hands to be washed and dried at the "drying machines." There were also paper towels to be strewn expressively over the floor. And, there were the mothers—advising, consenting, admonishing,—loving. There were also drinking fountains to be explored. There was the Ticket Man to be annoyed, an isolated conductor or two to be quizzed. And, best of all, there were the ponderous trains to be observed, commented upon, and stared at with awesome respect.

There were so many and varied things to occupy one's attention at the Train Station, but, as always, the inevitable finally happened:

"Mrs. Mackin," Clifford wanted to know, "when do we eat?"

"This—right here—would be a good place," Mrs. Mackin answered, observing bench after bench of unoccupied waiting-room space.

"The children could sit here and I could pass the sand..." then she stopped abruptly.

"My God! Where is Justin?" She spoke in a frozen cotton-candy kind of whisper.

"Here!" she hissed, shoving the sandwich suitcase at me. Then, taking off through the station like a horizontal rocket—misfired—, she disappeared.

I hurriedly counted heads and whispered directions to the other mothers.

"Mrs. Jackson and Mrs. Richards, remain with the children," I ordered, as though I lost a kid every day.

"Mrs. Burnett and Mrs. Williamson—come with me."

"Fan out," I further directed, "there aren't many places he could be. The Greentree Station isn't that big," I said reassuringly.

"What does Justin look like?" Mrs. Burnett asked, bewildered.

"He'll be a boy—alone," I replied.

And we all threw up our arms and dispersed.

Mrs. Williamson, without batting an eyelash disappeared through the door marked "MEN'S ROOM" while Mrs. Burnett, after resembling an ostrich viewing an indecisive, directionless butterfly, went at last in search of a drinking fountain where she thought all little boys should congregate.

I, realizing how very interested Justin was in science and engineering, decided to head straight for the trains and tracks again and pushed through the big wooden doors that led to the yards.

The noise there was now one steaming, straining, bursting backfire—or whatever trains do. My eardrums strained in the din—strained against all the screeching, screaming grind of breaks and metal against metal.

"Justin," I tried calling, but of course it was useless.

One mammoth iron monster's wheels were beginning to turn...

"Chug...chug..." There!? Was that Justin's profile in the window???

"My God!" I suddenly thought, "Could Justin have boarded...?" the thought went through me like lye through goose grease...

"Justin! Justin!" I called helplessly, shifting the sandwich suitcase, which was weighing heavily now, to the other hand, and breaking into a dead run alongside of the gradually moving train.

My voice was a voice crying in a wilderness of heavy water vapor—crying in a desert of stark, raging noise.

Oh! How I ran! "Justin! get off that train at once!" I sobbed.

My legs were moving as fast as I could make them go, but they were aimless moving pedals—like so many arms on a multi-legged caterpillar. I was a puppy dog trying to make it on newly-waxed kitchen linoleum.

But suddenly from behind came a giant WHOOSH, and a gravelly voice gravelled:

"Don't worry, Lady, you'll make it! Here!" The "here" was the swooping down and the unburdening of the sandwich suitcase!

"STOP! STOP!" I screamed after the man. "I'm NOT GOING ANYWHERE!"

But my legs disproved the fact.

They were perpetual motion rudders on a run-away paddle boat,—they were the revolving spokes of a single-minded, single-purposed unicycle,—but they finally caught up with him.

"Mister!" I bellowed against the roar.

"Here, honey," he interrupted, grinning and shoving me back the suitcase.

"I'm not going any..." I started to shout, but I never finished.

Never Pluck a Persimmon

With one Herculean scoop I was hoisted suddenly into the air and over his shoulder! It was in this instant, too, that I could see the boy in the window *was not Justin*!

"Put me down!" I screamed. "I'm not going anywhere!"

"Here! Here! Here!" the porter consoled.

I was immediately set down onto the first set of moving steps that came by in the passing coach!

To steady myself I grabbed hold of the steel hand rail.

MY GOD! The landscape was leaving me!

Familiar sights were fast disappearing but I could make out the porter,—beaming now, and waving through the steam. His expression was "A Job Well Done."

I looked forlornly at the sandwich-suitcase and thought of all those hungry third-graders back in the station and wondered what their mothers could tell them about my making off with all the food.

How could I ever explain this to Mr. Birly?

The Station was now a mere speck on the horizon!

I shrugged resignedly to myself.

"Well," I mused, "I haven't had a train ride for a long time," and, carrying the suitcase with a more philosophic air, now, I set out to find a conductor—or whatever—to see if he had any suggestions.

XXI

GETTING READY

"The Dedication is just one day off now," I said to the class the next school day. I was deliberately changing the subject. We had been discussing our Class Trip and the youngsters as yet couldn't seem to grasp how a grown woman could be abducted and stranded at the same time—with their sandwiches.

I had tried the "Forgive and Forget" approach which went only so far, and while I felt that all had really and truly been forgiven, Justin Mackin—who had turned up a block from the station watching a steam shovel excavate a basement for a new house—was not going to let them forget.

"But what did you *really* do—with all those sandwiches?" he persisted.

I replied in a slow deliberate tone:

"Because I discovered that most of them had been made with mayonnaise—because they had been in the warm car and then of course, the warm train—(of course) I thought it best that they not be eaten—by us," I concluded.

"After all," I added cautiously, "we could get sick—eating mayonnaise that has not been kept refrigerated." It took me quite a while before the engineer agreed to stop the train. Then the taxi back...and..."

I kept my calm.

"Now," I continued, "what actually happened to them is this: I threw them away. I didn't want you to get sick.. And, I returned the suitcase to Justin's mother."

"Now—about the Dedication," I went on.

"Most of you will be here tomorrow night at the Centennial gymnasium first and then, later, here at Sesqui. I want you to be on your best behavior."

A hand went up.

It was Clifford.

"But my mother won't let me go to the Dedication without a haircut," he whined. "And she works and can't take me to the barber shop. And my

Dad works—on the road, and he won't be home until after the Dedication is over."

"Well," I thought ahead, "I've got all the refreshments lined up for tomorrow night," I plotted. "If your mother would like me to accompany you to the barber's, have her call me after school and I'll take you." And it was settled.

I was elected to escort Sir Clifford to his hairdresser's that very afternoon—after school. And so it was that Clifford and I sought out a tonsorial artist along Greentree's main drag.

But, when we arrived at the peppermint-stick pole Mrs. Richards had pointed out, we discovered a small sign in the door which announced that the proprietor had gone ice fishing in Upper Michigan and would be not only gone for the day but for the rest of the week.

What to do? Clifford needed a haircut now.

Dejectedly, then, we turned toward the Greentree "downtown" in hopes of finding another shop.

We had walked the two blocks into downtown and we were now rapidly heading out of it when I spied a small cardboard red and white striped pole tacked inside a grimy window. Peering through the yellowy filmed glass, I did ascertain two barber chairs and mirrors, etc., and thus decided that although business did not look as though it had been booming, it might be possible to secure a haircut on the premises.

"Come on, Clifford," I suggested, "let's try this one," and we pushed open the old-fashioned, wooden, paint-peeling door.

We walked hesitantly over to a leathery sort of sofa that had as many cracks and wrinkles as a sun-addicted apricot and sat down.

The girly calendars were in evidence as were the dirty ash trays.. The odor of stale cigar smoke hung heavily in the air. And, the cheesecake magazines were all at least eight months old!

"The place has gone to pot," I thought. To Clifford I said:

"We'll only wait a minute more. If no one comes to cut your hair we'll take off."

It was all right with Clifford.

But then a creaky door to the rear of the establishment suddenly opened and a grey-haired, benevolent-looking man appeared. He poked his head into the barber shoppe proper like a ground hog looking furtively for his shadow.

"Oh," he said, surprised at seeing customers. "Did you want something?"

Judging from Clifford's fringed-lampshade appearance I thought his question was aimed solely at making conversation.

"A hair-cut," I smiled.

"Fine," he said. "I'll be with you in one moment." And he disappeared again—from whence he came.

Five more minutes of waiting but then he came, carrying a pair of scissors the size of something left over from the Reign of Terror.

"Come," he motioned to Clifford.

Clifford went, but it seemed to me that his feet dragged.

"Where are your electric clippers?" Clifford asked somewhat concerned.

Judging from the look of the place I doubted if it had electricity.

"Never use them," tho barber answered.

And Clifford mounted his throne. He was subsequently draped in a section of roughly-torn white sheet that had never had even a nodding acquaintance with bleach. He looked like a little impoverished monarch, struggling desperately to keep body and kingdom together.

And the snipping began. Hesitant clip, clips here—a sporadic slice there—with the comb held for guidance, direction—or whatever. But it was not the clipping itself that made me sit up onto the very edge of that cracked leather sofa. The old man's hands were shaking to such an extent that I became immediately concerned about Clifford's eyes.

As the barber headed toward the front of Clifford's head I whispered:

"Clifford, don't move. Don't even blink."

Clifford apparently, puzzled about all the palsy, or whatever, asked:

"Miss Morrow, are there many earthquakes around here?"

"Who would ever come in here for a haircut," I asked myself. You took your life in your hands. But then again, perhaps the old man was starving for lack of customers. Perhaps he shook from weakness.

And the clip, clips went on. I could hardly believe it.

The old man was shaking Clifford's hair now, onto the floor,—from the tattle-tale gray sheet that had protected his clothing.

I took a cursory look at Clifford—half afraid to accept now the reality of the situation.

Clifford did indeed look like The Last of the Mohicans—sidewise!

Never Pluck a Persimmon

I didn't know what to say. Clifford, fortunately, had not looked in a mirror.

"What do I owe you?" Clifford was saying manfully, rattling the change in his pocket.

"Seventy-five cents," the man said, still shaking the hair from the cloth.

"Seventy-five cents!" Clifford bellowed! "WOW! You're cheap!"

The old man stopped shaking. He turned to me, a quizzical look on his face.

"What do they...they charge for haircuts—now?" he addressed me.

"I don't know," I truthfully answered. "I just don't know."

"You've a small head!" he turned back to Clifford. "Seventy-five cents!"

Clifford counted out the money and, at the last nickel's emergence from his knee-deep pocket, the back door to the barbershop burst open and a huge hulk of a man—a man with a ruddy complexion—stood, surprised and baffled at our presence...

"What th...?" he started to say.

"Why, Mr. Herendeen. HELLO!" I greeted.

"Hello," he flushed. "What're ya doin' here?" He looked a bit angry.

"Why, we're getting a haircut," I nodded to Clifford. "Clifford's mother wouldn't let him go to the Dedication tomorrow night if we didn't get him a haircut."

"Why..." Mr. Herendeen turned sharply to the old man. "You don't have good sense. What a risk you've taken. And...," Mr. Herendeen was aghast, "Look what you've done to that kid's hair. You'll have every cop in town after us now. Come on," Mr. Herendeen beckoned Clifford and me into the street.

"Honey," he said in whispered tones so Clifford could not hear. "That place is no barber shop. It's a front! It's a horse room—in the back."

"But..." I didn't understand.

"I doubt if Old Mo ever gave a haircut in his whole entire life before," Mr. Herendeen continued. After shooting a glance at Clifford he blurted:

"I'm sure of it. Wait til his mother gets a load o' _that_. The cops will swoop down on that place like flies on a manure pile."

"But...but, Mr. Herendeen," I still was not satisfied. "What were _you_ doing in there...—in the back room?"

"Me?" he cleared his throat. "Why, I'll level with you. I was playing the horses. I'm having trouble livin' on a teacher's salary. Me with five kids and all."

"But..." I still persisted.

"Will you get in any trouble...for...for...playing the horses in there?"

"No," he reassured. "But don't go tellin' Mr. Birly on me. I never play them on school time."

"Of course not," I answered, a little hurt that Mr. Herendeen had forgotten that I was a champion of lost causes and underdogs—witness the tuxedo-give-away to the Union. Why should he think I would tell?

"Lissen," Mr. Herendeen said, getting an eyeful of Clifford again, "I cut my own boys' hair. Lissen, let's stop at my house and I'll trim you a bit."

Clifford immediately gave a moan. He was tired of all the grownups tinkering with his head.

"Ah-h-h-h-h," he started to say.

"Clifford, please," I begged. "If you—if you let Mr. Herendeen fix you up I'll—I'll buy you a black and white double dip cone."

"Ugh! No!" wailed Clifford.

"I'm sorry. I forgot. No chocolate," I reassured.

"Okay," Clifford grinned, "but I can't see why I have to get two haircuts in one day."

"Clifford," Mr. Herendeen turned him around by the shoulders. "If you want to avoid getting two haircuts instead of one, you must remember to never, never, never go to that Barber Shop—ever again, as long as you live," he added with finality.

"I wouldn't be caught dead in it again." He grinned up at Mr. Herendeen. "They don't even own a set of clippers."

"That's exactly my point," Mr. Herendeen said, finishing the conversation.

And the three of us headed for the Malt Shoppe.

"Be sure it's a double-dip—vanilla," Clifford reminded.

"Double Dip!" Mr. Herendeen said under his breath. "I think there's a Double Dipper in the seventh."

XXII

THE DEDICATION

February first dawned, a grey, ugly day—Dedication Day! Today the Superintendent would speak; the school children would perform; Sesqui would be honored. But now, since it was Sunday, church was the first thing on the agenda. And, oh, how I needed guidance and prayers!

Mr. Herendeen had finally taken the twenty-six tuxedos from my closet—the men had their fittings—and tonight the Jazz Combo would emerge from their former sloppy cocoons in spanking flashy tuxedos—but, (groan) exactly like the ones of A.G.H.A.S.T.'S Glee Club! If only I had had enough nerve to break down and tell Mr. Birly, my knees would not now be taking involuntary isometric exercises.

Mrs. Decklebaum and I attended the same church "of a Sunday morning" as Greentree-ers would say, and so we chit-chatted expectantly about the Dedication.

"Have the cookies held up all right dear?" she inquired, wondering if I had peeked into the freezer lately.

"They're fine and so is the punch. I'll only have to add water and ginger ale," I chattered. As we entered the church's white clapboard structure, our chatterings became whispers.

And forty-five minutes later, after Mrs. Decklebaum and I purchased some milk at the corner store for our coffee we were on our way home again.

"Greentree was a pretty place," I thought as we walked. There were so many lovely white oaks along the sidewalks. And maples, too. And even now, when they were bare they looked solid and dependable and had a dark expressive beauty all their own.

"God forbid!" Mrs. Decklebaum exclaimed as we rounded the last corner, "look at all the men standing in front of the house!"

I was not alarmed until I counted them. Sixteen! "Mrs. Decklebaum!! You couldn't have that many men cousins!" I told her. "There are at least sixteen!" They were leaning on the picket fence, against the elm tree—two were sitting on the front steps. One was, at the moment, spitting on the sidewalk.

As soon as we could see the whites of their eyes Mrs. Decklebaum called in a friendly-enough tone:

"Whatever are all of ye doin' here?"

This was indeed an odd assortment of men. Some were in their early twenties; some in their early thirties; some middle-aged. But all of them had a kind of earthy seediness about them as though they had really come to grips with the world.

"We're from Tintown," said the first one. "We've come for those tuxedos."

"Wh—wh—wh—," I started to say.

"We met a kid on the street. He took us to this house. Said the teacher who had them lived here."

"How did all of you ever get 'way up here?" Mrs. Decklebaum demanded, still somewhat uncomprehending.

"We came in a kind of anti-poverty truck," the one nearest answered with a smirk on his face. At this the men all laughed.

"We didn't all have to come," said another chomping on something. "But there was room." When he smiled, the lack of teeth came through, like a Jack O'Lantern ogling a Halloweener.

"What can we do?" my landlady put in, looking to me now for...for whatever...

"Look," I said to the most talkative one near me. "I can't give you those tuxedos because I won't have them until about 9:30 tonight. They're being worn by a Glee Club here in Greentree and by a Jazz Combo tonight from 7:30 to about 9:30.

"Now," I continued, "you could maybe find out more about them—about where you could pick them up and so on—by calling on Mr. Birly—Mr. Timothy Birly, the Principal of our Centennial School. His address is 110 Elm Street," I hardly came up for air. Fear kept me at it. Sixteen men wanting something you can't deliver!

"Elm Street is four blocks over and two up," I concluded, directing with my index finger. "you could walk it in five minutes."

"Where's your truck?" Mrs. Decklebaum asked suddenly.

"Getting a cup of coffee," said the leader.

"Okay, then," he added bowing slightly, "we'll see Mr. Birly," and, smirking again,"and thank ye for helpin.'" What was it about this man? Was he ridiculing us?

Never Pluck a Persimmon

Inside the house Mrs. Decklebaum proceeded to the refrigerator while I collapsed against her front door.

"In the name of the Good Lord," I thought, "how did things happen like this...?"

"But really," I said aloud, trying to salve my conscience. "Mr. Birly deserves this problem. He's the one who held up sending those...those tuxedos. Now he can tell them why he never sent them..."

"You're so right, dear. But what is Mr. Birly going to do with sixteen men all day? He'll be needin' to get things done for the Dedication, too." Mrs. Decklebaum mused. "Maybe he could invite them to the Dedication!" She added.

Mrs. Decklebaum was unreasonable!

"Invite them!" I fairly shouted.

"Well, what else?" Mrs Decklebaum shrugged, reaching for the coffee pot.

The pot had hardly issued a perk when the phone rang:

"Miss Morrow," Mr. Birly stated a fact again. "It was so kind of you to send me these men from Tintown," he hissed into the phone. "What am I to do with them? Have you any suggestions as to how we can entertain <u>sixteen</u> men for <u>ten</u> hours?"

"<u>We</u>?" I was indignant.

Then I suggested:

"What about Mrs. Birly? Can't she think of something?"

"She's feeding them right now," he said as though he himself had been sucking on a lemon.

"Miss Morrow," Mr. Birly continued, "I'm counting on your helping with them at the Dedication," he added. "Show them around. It's their first big trip to a sizable town."

"I don't know," I said unconvinced. "One of them has eyes that look as though he's been plenty around.

"But," I added, "I'll try to help, Mr. Birly." I wanted to be sure of my job.

"When the men are finished with the tuxedos—our men—will we just pack them there and...?"

"I'm not looking that far ahead," Mr. Birly whispered now into the phone. "I'm sending them to a movie shortly—down at the Police Station. The cop on duty's hobby is cinematography."

"Wonderful!" I cried. That would take care of a couple of hours. Our conversation finished, then, I hung up the phone.

And that was the last I heard of the men from Tintown until that evening when I carried the punch bowl into Centennial for the festivities.

"I'll help ya'," a youngish-one said the same moment he snatched the crystal bowl from my all-encompassing arms, and, while my heart tipped straight up, he banged his way through the doors and onto the gymnasium floor.

Mr. Hubbard, the custodian, seeing so much willing manpower in evidence, did seize upon the opportunity and had the Tintown men put up the chairs inside the Centennial gym and then outside beside Sesqui for the brief ceremonies there.

The men's appearance, however, was exceedingly out of place. Whether or not the men had better clothes back home was not known, but the fact remains that they had not dressed for an occasion as formal as a Dedication in Greentree, and the black turtleneck sweaters and the fatigues and the pullover with the words "ONE HELLUVA GUY" did not blend in with the staid surroundings which now were including ribboned rosettes on the chairs along the aisles as well as huge buttons and bows tacked onto the gym's stage curtain.

"Oh well..." I thought, "how were they to know they'd have to wait for the tuxedos?..."

The microphones were put in place—the speakers' chairs set up. Soon the A.G.H.A.S.T. Glee Club director was also on the scene—arranging, re-arranging...

And the people dribbled in—and then they came in droves and at 7:25 it looked as though Sesqui would be having an honest-to, gosh-darn, genuine Dedication.

The Jazz Combo's amplifiers were also in place, as were the cookies on pretty silver trays. Mr. and Mrs. Birly were there smiling...But where was Superintendent Holmes?

The Tintown man called Curly was the one who kept pressing things.

"When do we get the tuxedos?" he asked through his toothpick, the minute Mr. Birly appeared wearing his. His, of course, was very much up-to-date.

"This...th...this is not one of them," Mr. Birly said looking down to make sure.

"This is my own."

Never Pluck a Persimmon

Curly understood.

"You'll get the tuxedos just as soon as everything is over and the men can wriggle out of them, Curly," Mr. Birly assured him. "Now why don't you go get a cookie?"

"I've had ten," Curly answered, "but okay, I'll get another one."

There was no trumpet-pronouncement. Just a few clearings of throats and the Dedication began.

The flower girls came first,—girls from Centennial's fourth and fifth grades,—with ferns in their hair and wallpaper-covered fruit boxes filled with flower petals which they sprinkled lavishly all about them to the tune, "She Wore a Tulip".

In May now, I understood that the Greentree flower girls could have the wooden strawberry boxes filled with real blossoms, but in February they contained art-lesson scraps from Centennial and crepe paper strips from the 4-H Fair. But whatever they carried, the contents were soon strewn over the Centennial gym—possibly to make an honored path for Superintendent Holmes. But, now, no...he was already on the stage. Well, whatever...

The A.G.H.A.S.T. Glee Club marched in now and sang their entire repertoire of Cole Porter. Hoosiers were loyal to Hoosiers. The women's black gowns were lovely. And the men did look proper, and even prosperous in their dignified tuxedos. Also, they all looked very much up-to-date in spite of those large lapels and padded shoulders. And how they were applauded! And how Mr. Birly beamed! It was good to see him happy. And how the men from Tintown seemed to watch each man wearing a tuxedo's every move! It was evident they were not going to let the merchandise get away.

"I never thought the Tintowners...well..." my thinking was interrupted.

The eighth grade girls had started their Oral Presentation.

"The Night to Remember"—meaning the Dedication night, started in grave sombre tones with four girls holding the title on four large placards. I discovered later the the piece had been called "A Night to Remember" but the mother of the girl who had to carry the "A" on her bosom, thinking of Hester Prynne's ordeal, objected. It was therefore changed to "The" which made it all very proper.

But now, according to the program, it was time for the G.O.T. Jazz Combo. My heart skipped a beat as the G.O.T. men finally revealed themselves—in identical fancy attire as the A.G.H.A.S.T. men-singers.

The secret life of Miss Morrow was now exposed! Before the very eyes of Mr. Birly!

The instrumentalists all walked confidently across the stage as Mr. Herendeen, seizing upon the drama of the moment, started to applaud. The ripple of applause became a generous out-pouring of hands. It was almost as though G.O.T. had finally come of age and been accepted and here were many A.G.H.A.S.T.-inians APPROVING of them!

"Well now—by gum—they *had* class!" the clapping declared. I desperately tried to catch Mr. Birly's reaction to the G.O.T. "New Look" but all I could make out was the back of his neck from which several veins looked as though they might be protruding. But I could see Mrs. Birly nudge her husband and clap in a good sportsmanship fashion. Good for her!

"Why look, Daddy,—those men are just like you!" said a little one nearby whose father had sung with A.G.H.A.S.T.

"From the mouths of angels," I was thinking as the Jazz Combo opened up and sent the Demons of Sound flying in all directions.

In seconds, the place jumped. Even Superintendent Holmes, whose speech was next, smiled, and then started his foot with the beat.

For the next five minutes all present were glad they had come. This was fun! They clapped their hands, jiggled their feet, and winked mischievously at one another. The only thing that disturbed me at the moment was the sight of ten Tintown men near the refreshment spread—chewing on their cookies in time with the music. At that rate..

"Oh, well..." I thought, "perhaps they're still hungry. Mrs. Birly may not have had enough in the house to feed them properly..."

Fortunately for everyone, since it was rather anti-climactic after such music, Superintendent Holmes kept his words short. He did, however, ask everyone in the place to take themselves now out the door and over to Sesqui for the "official" dedication. As Sesqui's teacher, I was presented with a large beautiful bouquet of red roses and told to be seated on the platform that had been erected for the occasion—in front of Sesqui.

"Be sure to wear your coats," an usher with a feeling-for-humanity spoke into the microphone.

A raw February wind had been whipping about when we had first entered Centennial. There was no real reason to believe that at 8:50 it had abated. And, we discovered, it had not.

Never Pluck a Persimmon

Because the Sesqui part of the program was to be understandably short, there were fewer folding chairs arranged than were actually needed. Many of the townspeople stood in the cold, silent wind. And some who sat suddenly stood.

"Could it be that the metal chairs were unbearably cold?" I thought.

"Why didn't they have this back in October?" said an irate woman, putting up her fur collar, "or during the simmon festival?"

"It's not to be for long," her husband answered.

From the platform I was seeing for the first time that cookies and hot cocoa would have filled the bill better than cookies and cold punch.

But now the Jazz Combo was coming forward to play a little—to warm things up? And Superintendent Holmes was ready to take over.

He took the microphone now and said something about "on this great occasion"—and then he said something about "a clever touch" and left the platform all in good humor.

It was here that Mr. Herendeen, wearing one of the left-over tuxedos and looking very handsome and healthy in it, took the microphone to explain:

"G.O.T. has a surprise for you all," he said happily.

"It was one of our creative member's ideas. The Superintendent will tell you about it."

"Here I am," the Superintendent then called into a portable mike. "I'm down here by the big elm tree—far enough away from the persimmons," he laughed.

"And I'm going to christen Sesqui for us all! The bottle of champagne is all ready!"

"Champagne would freeze in this..." but then I stopped thinking...

My 20-20 vision saw it all. There was a head. It was a head. It was Jeb Hinchey's, sticking out from a man-sized, papier-maché, foil-wrapped 'bottle'—up in the elm tree! He was lowering himself now so that, I supposed, the Superintendent would be able to 'swing' him.

"There's one tux we didn't need," I thought consolingly to myself.

Jeb Hinchey didn't need a tux. He was all bottle! But someone was now lighting something at the base of that bottle. The drums in the Combo were rolling now, a dramatic, all-embracing crescendo.

The Superintendent was giving a preliminary swing and then Jeb was headed straight in our direction with something coming from the bottom of his bottle.

Sparks! And then a cascade! As Jeb landed on the platform I could see that two "fountains"—fireworks—had been strapped to his bottom to give the effect of water flowing for the christening.

How clever! And if the fuses had been just millimeters longer the timing would have been perfect!

The people laughed and clapped loudly in appreciation.

"And now," Mr. Hiram Rompers, President of the Union was saying, "before Mr. Toothaker presents the President of the School Board, Mr. John Calhoun Jones, with the generous check—to have Sesqui connected—we have a few more fireworks, donated by the Kwongyuen Hangkee Manufacturers in Macau to give us a preview of what is available for July 4th.

And then suddenly there was a flashing, brilliantly-colored and sparkling George Washington crossing the Delaware, followed by an Abraham Lincoln, and Uncle Sam and a beautiful waterfall which had been mistakenly placed upside-down on the ground. The result of all this then was an illuminated Old Faithful!

The people, and particularly the children, responded wholeheartedly. When the rockets were sent heavenward everyone cheered. The majority now even forgot about the cold. They stomped their feet and "ooooooooohed" and "aa-aa-aa-aahed" appreciatively. A special note was added by one of the Tintown men who now jostled the Jazz Combo drummer aside and started to "perform" as the rockets and fireworks danced. Here was an accomplished drummer who knew just what sound effects a hurling Roman candle needed and who understood implicitly the swish of a sky-rocket. He—this Tintown man—even knew to roll when a firecracker fizzled embarrassedly on the grass. What perception!

But something was wrong! What was it? Mrs. Jackson was whispering something into my ear. She had braved the walking up on the platform to do so:

"Miss Morrow," she almost spoke, "my husband is missing!"

"Missing!" I was uncomprehending. "How could he be missing?" I was shouting now above the drum roll.

"We were over there," she pointed, "watching Abraham Lincoln and I turned around and he was gone!"

"Where's Robert?" I wanted to know.

"Robert is looking for his Father," she said, very near to tears.

Never Pluck a Persimmon

Before I could even think of something to say Mrs. Birly reached the foot of the platform calling wildly:

"MISS MORROW. MR. BIRLY IS MISSING! HAVE YOU SEEN HIM?"

Mr. Jackson missing was a tragedy. But Mr. Birly missing was a calamity!

"How could the Rock of Gibraltar be missing?" I asked myself. I quickly placed my roses onto the chair while the fireworks continued in rapid succession and while the drums with the Tintown man the center of attention continued to beat. I left the platform in search of the missing men.

It was, however, when the huge American flag was lit, and when Mrs. Helderlein, the soprano from the First Christian Church broke out into "God Bless America"—transposed to a higher key—that Mrs. Richards, Mrs. Birly and myself discovered we were not alone.

"Have you seen my husband?" Mrs. Williamson, Mary Jane's mother, wanted to know, snuggling her nose into her lamb's wool. From the added light from the flag I could see that the audience was in a state of flux. Spectators were no longer watching—nor standing still. They were moving about uneasily as though looking for something...or...someone...And there was something different now. There was an odd stillness in spite of Mrs. Helderlein's singing. The drum had ceased its beating—could this be it? But of course it must be in deference to Mrs. Helderlein's singing. Yet...

A SCREAM! A SHRILL, PENETRATING, ALL-SHATTERING SCREAM suddenly rent the cold February air.

"My God!" the woman shouted. "Help my husband!"

And all Greentree took off in the direction of the scream.

I pushed behind the clump of bushes now...I pushed to the very edge of the circle there—to help?...to see...to...

I did not know the husband. I did not know the woman who screamed—the wife. But I did know that seeing a man with a rag stuffed in his mouth and his hands tied behind him in his unadorned underwear with skinny hairy legs exposed to the February elements—this is a pitiful sight!

"One helluva fella—One helluva fella!" the man mumbled when the rag was removed.

"Those Tintown fellas!" he gasped, "took the tuxedo off me...and my wallet," he felt his underwear, "It's gone!"

Just now Mrs. Helderlein reached the "to the ocean, white with foam" part, but that's as far as she ever got.

"LADEEZ AND GENTLEMEN," someone said most solemnly into the microphone:

"HOLD ON TO YOUR PANTS. I REPEAT. HOLD ONTO YOUR PANTS. AND YOUR WALLETS..."

It sounded like Mr. Birly! I pushed my way out of the circle.

It WAS Mr. Birly—and in his undershirt and shorts or b.v.d.'s—or whatever—standing, proclaiming, warning.

"I have been stripped and robbed," he continued with the understatement of the year in much the same tone as though he had said:

"An artichoke is a vegetable and you better believe it."

At this point Mr. Hiram Rompers, the G.O.T. president, in long, loose-hanging, underwashed underwear panted onto the platform.

Before he could utter a syllable Mr. Birly pointed his index finger:

"HE has been stripped and robbed!" and thus informed the astounded spectators of this new situation.

"We have all been stripped and robbed," shouted Mr. Jeremy White—husband of Mrs. White, A.G.H.A.S.T.'s President—from his shorts. He jumped onto the platform then from the other end and shrieked the latest:

"My wife has gone to notify the Police!" and he folded his arms in an anti-shiver pose.

"They're on the lookout right now for their truck!"

There was something very symbolic about that mottled assortment on the platform. There they were! The Union and the Association together,—previously in finery, now together again in unmerited disgrace. Both together! Both shivering! Both suffering—one for all and all for one, down underneath where the underwear was.

And now they were being given things—just anything—to bundle in. Mr. Birly plunged into his wife's sweater and detachable fur cape like a seal diving for salmon. Mr Herendeen on the other hand was seen momentarily slinking away in the tablecloth I had borrowed from Mrs. Decklebaum for the occasion.

But now Mr. Toothaker, Treasurer of the P.T.A. strode up, fully clothed, to present the check to get Sesqui connected. He still had the check and he waved it over his head.

Never Pluck a Persimmon

But who could care? Mr. Toothaker after some effort couldn't find the President of the Board, John Calhoun Jones, to give him the check.

Who was interested?

No one was even watching. The facts were, if your husband still had his pants you headed for the car, gratefully counting your blessings and glad to get the heater running. If your husband's tuxedo had been taken from him and he had been "rolled" you got him huddled into the Centennial pay phone while he flexed and unflexed his muscles, or you shoved him into a stall in the Men's or Ladies' Room until you could think of something and until he could thaw out. Most of the time, however, he just sat there despondent at his failure to successfully defend himself and save his wallet, and he never cared to come out at all.

With sixteen Tintowners on the prowl the damage they evoked in a few unsuspecting minutes on the residents of Greentree was exceedingly great.

The Dedication which had begun on such a high jubilant tone, ended on an all-time low.

As I picked up my beautiful roses—now limp from being neglected on the metal folding chair and resisting the cold—my eyes looked over to Sesqui.

"So who cared—tonight—or any night—if it got connected or not?" I addressed the problem. "Men gave their all, and what did it matter?" I asked myself. Sesqui stood aloof and unconcerned in the bitter February night.

"Care if I walk you home?" the voice said in my ear.

It was Jeb Hinchey, still the champagne bottle!

"Sure, Jeb," I said, sensing that his fizz was all gone, too.

"I guess I won't get the prize for collecting the most clothes now for the Clothing Drive, Jeb," I said, to fill up the empty air.

"Those tuxedos are dispersed across the country-side," I continued aimlessly—"strewn to the winds...and the wallets with them."

"Some of the tuxedos could still be in the truck," Jeb added consolingly. "But I doubt it. They would have been much more interested in the contents of the wallets..."

"Tintown..." Jeb started to say.

"To hell with Tintown!" I said with finality, fighting tears.

I was certain that if champagne bottles had been designed with arms, Jeb Hinchey could have found a use for at least one of them.

XXIII

THE BIRTHDAY PARTY

"Miss Morrow, now, about Unita's party that's comin' up," Clifford introduced his subject again. "My mother will be writing you a note about it. It will be about <u>no chocolate</u>," he added.

"All right, Clifford. You bring it in. I shall read it," I said feigning patience.

It was a gloomy Monday morning and Clifford was adding to it.

In the first place there were no Weekly Bulletins in our mail boxes over in Centennial. The Weekly Bulletin did serve the purpose of keeping the teachers informed—day by day—of assemblies, the nurse's hours for the week, the time when the Art Supervisor would be around, etc. In other words the Weekly Bulletin kept you on your toes. But this particular Monday Mr. Birly apparently didn't care which part of their anatomy his teachers were operating on. After the Dedication Pandemonium—well, Mr. Birly didn't care. It was apparent that he had lost heart when not one single solitary communique came over the "wire"—the ingenious pulley device of Mrs. Puternaugh's.

I did not know, for instance, until I read it in the Greentree Times that Mr. Toothaker did finally present the P.T.A. check for Sesqui to Mr. John Calhoun Jones, but only after Mr. Jones was located in the far petunia patch hiding behind some masonry, aware that, indeed, some dire plot was underway. The check, the paper said, came to the tremendous grand total of $1,632!!!

Greentree had a right to be proud of itself!

The paper did not say, however, when work would begin or whether or not bids would be opened or whether or not there would be more meetings to determine the size of the Sesqui bathroom—whether the Sesqui closet should be enlarged—or whether an addition should be built.

There were many things up in the air this gloomy Monday morning. And one was, as Clifford kept reminding me, Unita's party.

"Cupcakes are easy to handle," I advised Unita. "Be sure to tell your mother."

"Tell her no chocolate ones, too," Clifford put in.

Never Pluck a Persimmon

"Clifford, this does not concern you," I scolded, hoping his hair would soon be back to normal. Mr. Herendeen had done and admirable "patch" job but Clifford still resembled a porcupine with the mod look from the punk-rockers of London.

That afternoon, Clifford, true to his word, brought the note:

Dear Miss Morrow,
    Clifford tells me that Unita will be having a birthday party this Wednesday afternoon, and he is afraid to come to school for fear Unita's mother plans to serve chocolate cake and chocolate ice cream. I told him I thought there would be vanilla. However, Clifford is to have no chocolate of anything. It upsets him terribly if he eats it.
    Will you kindly see to it then that in case Unita's mother brings chocolate cake or ice cream that Clifford has none of it? I will send Clifford a package of life-savers that afternoon so that he has something to suck on, in case.
Sincerely,

P.S. Also, what did you say was the name of that barber again?
P.P.S. Also, Clifford says that once in September you made him drink chocolate milk. Clifford never forgets.
Sincerely again.
Mrs. Richards

The answer to Mrs. Richards was ready for Clifford when he went home at 3:00 p.m. No poetry. Only diplomacy.

Dear Mrs. Richards,
    I assure you I will see to it that Clifford does not get anything chocolate the day of the party. Mothers, thinking of the pretty dresses of the girls and the nice, clean shirts of the boys, bring vanilla, to my knowledge, 90% of the times. But I will certainly see to it that Clifford is protected and kept from anything chocolate.
    Yes, it is true that Clifford drank a half-pint carton of chocolate milk in September (before I knew of his aversion to it) but Clifford *volunteered* to drink this, in addition to his daily white carton of H

& H pure, homogenized milk, and I distinctly remember this because, being a new teacher and all, he frightened me. After consuming the chocolate carton he announced to the class:

"I think I'm going to explode!" and then he told us that he is forbidden anything chocolate, too late.

Understandingly,
Miss Morrow

As I sealed the envelope I discovered Mr. Jackson at Sesqui's door.

"Miss Morrow," he began, "may I see you a minute?" he asked, and I ushered him into Sesqui proper and then into Sesqui's closet which he said he wanted to measure.

"I'm discouraged," he confided, kneeling with his measuring tape inside the narrow confines of the closet. "We've not had one official word from the School Board on when they plan to start getting Sesqui connected. They're just not saying anything."

"Did you see *The Times* editorial last evening?" I asked him, trying to see the bright side.

"About Sesqui being an innovation in education and a regression in civilization?" Mr. Jackson asked. "Yes, I saw it. And we need more of them. But," and he shook his head, "I thought all the foundations had already been laid. I thought they'd be here Monday morning starting on the pipes." Then he dropped his lip: "Why, they haven't even told me which plumber they've approved of yet."

"But it's still early, Mr. Jackson," I tried to reassure. "People aren't over the Dedication yet."

"That's true," Mr Jackson commented, remembering that he, too, lost his trousers and his billfold, also.

"Oh-h-h-h, if they ever catch up with those thieves!" I clenched my fists.

"They've never found one trace of those fellas, have they?" Mr. Jackson wanted to know.

"No," I commented sadly, "but I'd like to be around when they bring them to justice."

"Well," Mr. Jackson said, getting to his feet, "I have my measurements."

"And I have mine," I thought to myself.

Never Pluck a Persimmon

And he was gone—a dejected-looking figure silhouetted against the grey, grey sky. After all, how long was his kid supposed to put up with primitive conditions like this—and after he had worked so hard to improve things.

"Remember, Unita," Clifford was now saying, on his way back from the pencil sharpener, "if your mother brings chocolate ice cream my mother is going to be mad."

"Clifford!" I called him to my desk.

"Clifford," I continued, "I have had it. Now you mind your own business. I'm sick of hearing about this chocolate. This is Unita's party. It is Unita's birthday..."

"But it's my stomach," he protested.

"Clifford," I said, steeling myself, "when you are forty years of age you will no doubt be a very nice man. However," and I paused for breath and strength, "God help those who have to put up with you until then."

I breathed again and continued:

"Now go to your seat. Stay there until it is time for dismissal. And if you have something to say you must raise your hand."

And the grey skies matched my mood.

And another grey dawned—Wednesday, party day, Unita's birthday. Before the hour that school convened, first a barrage of hailstones hit Greentree, followed by a violent rainfall which gradually receded as it changed to snow.

But Unita's mother sent all the right things! She could not come herself, the note explained, because she worked as a waitress at a Greentree Cafe but she hoped I wouldn't have any trouble. There were beautiful pink and white frosted cupcakes in a compact carton—*vanilla* ice cream cups packed in dry ice, and a favor for each child—lovely miniature embroidered bean bags! How very different! They were hand-made! And even Clifford seemed pleased with these.

When the penmanship lesson was finished the party began.

First the third graders played a kind of Bird Bingo, with paper silver stars as prizes—then a musical chair game, and finally a "Put the Flower in the Flower Pot," a pin-the-tail-on-the-donkey type of thing. And then it was refreshment time.

It was turning into a lovely party! But Clifford managed to change the tone of all this.

Virginia Morrow Black

    Before each little one emerged from Sesqui into the soft, feather-flakes that were now tumbling down on Greentree, before Unita was given the special "Birthday-girl" final send-off, before any of the bean bags were tucked safely against the tiny bosoms for safe-keeping on their way home from school—before any of this all happened...

                              Clifford,
              after eating one pink and *white* cupcake,
                                 and
               one vanilla *white* ice cream cup
                           THREW UP!;
                             1. on himself
                             2. on two other children
                             3. on the lemony-beige rug,
                        at Sesqui,
                 of Sesqui-Centennial
        of Greentree, Indiana—population 12,000
                           U.S.A.

    And Mrs. Richards, solicitous Mother of Clifford Richards, was duly informed of this dire happening—with Mr. Birly's blessing:

Dear Mrs. Richards:
    Clifford had his cupcake (white).
        Then he had his cream.
    Everything was white as snow—
        A big vanilla dream.
    But all of this came to an end
        (And he was *not* rebuked).
    But on the rug, and Dick and Jane—
        CLIFFORD RICHARDS PUKED!"

XXIV

THE BIG SNOW

By the time another week went by, with still no official word from the School Board about getting at the job of getting Sesqui connected, the pro-Sesqui townspeople were confused. Hadn't John Calhoun Jones, the President of the Board, been in favor of connecting Sesqui? Hadn't Mrs. Davis, Board Member, who lived directly across the street from Centennial, openly declared her loyalty on the side of Sesqui? Why was she silent now? Hadn't the money been raised and turned over to the Proper Authorities? Hadn't Mr. Jackson worked his fingers to the bone...? Hadn't Mr. Herendeen tried...? The P.T.A. Committee...?

The reason, according to Mr. Birly, who tried to assuage some of us was that Greentree was still in a state of shock over the Tintown Tuxedo escapade.

"When men's pockets have been picked at a school function," he explained to me in a numb kind of way, "it takes time for these men to forgive and forget. Let sleeping dogs lie—for the time being," he advised.

But needless to say the sleeping dog reared its head and growled ferociously when a strange telegram arrived from Tintown:

DEAR MR. BIRLY,
    TUXEDOS HAVE NOT YET ARRIVED STOP PLEASE ADVISE...

"Wh...wh...wh...," I began to say to Mr. Birly who sat looking as though he had dreamed up the whole Dedication mess after he had read the message.

"Wh...wh...wha...," he answered back.

"Mr. Birly," the thought sent shivers and quakes into my spine, "do you think...do you suppose those men weren't from Tintown?"

"I have just been on the phone with the police from that county," Mr. Birly spoke like the Ghost of Christmas Past. "They firmly believe the men couldn't have been Tintowners. Tintowners never leave Tintown," they say, "for any reason." Mr. Birly paused for breath...

Virginia Morrow Black

"Those men, according to the police, were bandits—some were transient carnival workers who were going through Tintown on their way south. They probably picked up the story about the tuxedos the whole town was awaiting," Mr. Birly was so crestfallen.

"Oh!" his words were slowly sinking in... "Mr. Birly! We have certainly mis-judged the people of Tintown, haven't we?" I offered.

"We have done just that," Mr. Birly conceded. "Well," he added on a brighter note, "we did send them many boxes of clothing. We still have a few tuxedos to send, too," he added hopefully. "And we've picked up a few here and there—off the lawns—and in the woods—some in shreds, but some are usable, with cleaning and pressing."

I nodded.

"And," Mr. Birly continued, "it seems all the G.O.T. people escaped with their pants intact. It was only the Association who lost theirs. I took note of that," and Mr. Birly looked knowingly into my baby-blue eyes.

"G.O.T. men know how to fight," he commented, weighing his words slowly. "Well," he added, "we'll send what we can." And then he concluded our little discussion, "That's all anyone can do."

I had never seen Mr. Birly so depressed. I decided to let the Sesqui-being-connected matter drop permanently for the time being.

But the *Greentree Times* would not let the matter vanish to oblivion. Mr. Jackson had sought out the roving reporter on Main Street and when asked what he believed to be <u>the</u> world crisis today, was quoted as saying:

"It is the struggle for freedom and independence against great odds. Small entities must fight against tyranny and oppression."

Mr. Jackson was gaining a suaveness with words he had never possessed before the Sesqui endeavor. But only a handful of citizens realized that he was talking about Sesqui and Centennial. The editorial in the same issue, however, was more specific:

> A great mass of wrongs is being inflicted on the tiny inhabitants of Sesqui—and there is no lifting of these wrongs in sight. Since when is a persimmon tree of more value than one of Greentree's own little pupils?
>
> Do we proceed with pipes and plumbers or do we destroy the trees and place Sesqui in her rightful place in the sun—directly beside Centennial's restrooms?

Never Pluck a Persimmon

>Let us unite in this grave cause. United we may yet produce spirit enough to lead us forward—to call forth a Lexington, to fight a Bunker's Hill, to drive the foe from the city of our rights!

They were strong words, fightin' words, but they went absolutely nowhere. Sesqui and Centennial went on as usual. No one had even a comment to make to the Voice of the People column concerning Sesqui's facilities or lack of them. No one even seemed to care. And still the School Board maintained its silence.

And the February doldrums swung into higher gear for March, but they were the doldrums just the same.

But these same higher-geared doldrums did blow in a lulu of a snowstorm which eventually succeeded in stirring the Greentree community to a bubbling, boiling, broiling cauldron.

The snow started simply enough—a feeble feathery covering of flakes at first that no one, not even the usual alarmists, viewed with suspicion. It was the first Thursday afternoon in March when it all began, and March was to usher in spring, and who took a pre-spring snowstorm seriously? By Friday morning, however, after the weather man had awakened to the fact that sixteen inches had already accumulated during the night and the end was nowhere in sight, the TV announcers and radiomen were listing the school-closings. The children were being told to stay home although no advice at all was given to the teachers. There were no paths open on any of the sidewalks where the children would be walking since no one could keep up with the fast-falling snow. Snow plows were working around the clock but they were breaking down, and with increasing rapidity, because of the extreme heaviness of the precipitation. But even though the snow presented problems, it <u>was</u> beautiful and I went out that evening to probe that beauty.

Walking past Centennial I discovered that the parking lot and playground there had not one shovel put to it as yet. And Sesqui? Where was it? That great hump there in the terrain? That muffled mound of mottled perseverance? Was that Sesqui?

It was—silently submitting itself to the inundating, overwhelming, absolute oblivion of the snow.

And Friday night gave no relief. In one unabated continuous stream, the frosty fragments kept coming. The measurement was now 24 inches of precipitation! Jehoshaphat!

Saturday had to be better. Greentree was in a state of emergency. The mail did not get through no matter what some people at the Post Office kept repeating...

It was evident that if relief did not come soon the schools would be closed again on Monday...

But I had forgotten about Greentree's slow-moving School Board—which was momentarily about to act with startlingly abrupt efficiency. The vigor, vitality, and verve they were to exhibit was, in essence, commendable, but the broken hearts their action left in the wake of the storm numbered into the hundreds and maybe the thousands.

The Board had taken so long to act on Sesqui that, well, the rapidity with which they responded to the snowstorm was breathtaking.

And the Greentree Times carried the whole story. And that story was straight from the horses' mouths. The School Board declared:

> Due to the snow crisis, education in Greentree is in a state of paralysis. Relief must come and it must be thorough. It must also be quick. Therefore, we the Board of Education appropriate the sum of $1632, to be spent immediately for emergency snow removal equipment. This equipment will be put to use as of this moment to alleviate the unfortunate conditions caused by the snow which, the Board feels, is a serious deterrent to learning.

There it was. In a few short sentences. All the blood, sweat and tears of all Sesqui-devotees—for naught.

And the snow plows rolled on and over my heart—all day Sunday. And Mrs. Decklebaum brought my coffee to me Monday morning and said:

"It's time for school dear. The children will be depending on you."

And I mustered my strength and my courage and pulled on my clothes and my shoe boots.

Grievous wrongs had been done! The little Satellite School's cup of forebearance and endurance was full! And it had been full for a long time.

Never Pluck a Persimmon

I rounded the corner. The new snow plows had done a tremendous job. Things had been beautifully cleared...The children could easily walk...But, "wh...wh...wh..." there, on my right. There stood stately, statuesque Centennial—but where, where was my little Sesqui? Where was the muffled mound of mottled perseverance? Where was the darling...the Apple of my Eye? The tiny appendage of Centennial?

Where Sesqui had once been—where the fun and laughter had echoed—there...there now remained only an empty space! One boldly bare desolate spot where the dirt now looked embarrassedly out from between the boundaries of Sesqui's previously-established dimensions!

I bewilderingly stood on the spot. On the hallowed spot—now. On the very spot.

It was plain as the nose on my face.

Sesqui's cup had finally spilled over into downright, outright, unquestionable, absolute rebellion!!!

The *Greentree Times'* announcement had it that Sesqui's resentment had simply boiled over.

"Sesqui has seceded," the headline read.

"SESQUI HAS SECEDED!"
And so it had!
And so it had!

XXV

THE WAR BETWEEN THE SCHOOLS

But, almost at the same moment I made my discovery—that Sesqui had certainly disappeared—I thought I ascertained her large tailights protruding from the clump of bushes on the property directly across from Centennial. Was it??? It was.

She had not gone far! Sesqui was parked right smack against School Board Member Cynthia Davis' substantial, nubby-bricked home. So! It was apparent that Mrs. Davis had not approved the majority vote!

"Well," I philosophized, "Sesqui had seceded but she was apparently still intact." I began the trek across the snow-scraped but still snow-covered street.

"Would the children see us...parked 'way over here?" I wondered. "And what would be the relationship now between Sesqui and Centennial considering these late developments? What would Mr. Birly say...and do...?"

Jehoshaphat! The world was suddenly filled with new problems!

As I walked nearer to the new premises I could see that the pro-Sesqui-ites, or whoever it was who took it upon themselves to move Sesqui—had also taken the time to decorate! Tree after tree and bush after bush on Mrs. Davis' property was strewn with a delicate, pastel-colored toilet tissue. The flamboyant message was apparent.

"Well," I said to myself at Sesqui's door now, "my key still fits Sesqui's lock anyway." For some reason I took this as a good sign. I then cautiously opened the door to the darkened classroom and snapped on the light. Of course nothing happened! The electric wires would have had to be snipped to cart Sesqui across the street!

And, in addition to the early-morning mid-winter semi-darkness I made another discovery. Br-r-r-r-r-r! Sesqui had no heat! In trying to connect Sesqui it had apparently been necessary to disconnect her!

Mrs. Davis was on Sesqui's doorstep.

"Miss Morrow, now never you mind," she began excitedly. "You just teach school like nothing has happened and you just remain neutral—no matter what. This argument is between me and the rest of the School Board and some irate townspeople...but you remain neutral," she repeated.

Never Pluck a Persimmon

"Neutral?" I thought. "How could I remain neutral when I was so dad-blasted cold?"

"Now never you mind," Mrs. Davis repeated, possibly seeing the blueness of my lips. "Mr. Herendeen is bringing a stove. And my husband will be running extension cords over for you any minute," she added encouragingly, "soon as he's up."

"Extension cords?" I thought I heard correctly.

"For the floor lamps. You need light!" she said exuberantly as though she would emulate the Creator on Creation Day.

"Let there be," I thought, resigning myself and bundling my coat around me.

"I hope Mr. Herendeen hurries up with that stove," I said aloud.

I had hardly finished the sentence when a ruffled roar cut directly across the Davis lawn to Sesqui. It was Mr. Herendeen, thank God, with Old Mo, the imposter-barber, *and* a pot-bellied stove.

"Here! Here, Miss Morrow, we'll have you all fixed up in a minute," Mr. Herendeen called.

"Please hurry!" I said to myself. And they began lugging in the crudest-looking, most cumbersome-seeming iron monstrosity I had ever seen. After the stove came the wood—then some coals—a small shovel—a poker—the entire works! Finally, then, a match was put to the innards and a roaring fire was a reality!

"This is from my Barber Shop," Old Mo explained to me, satisfied, when he was finished with everything. "Don't really need it," he affirmed, stating an honest fact. "Glad to help you out."

"Mr. Herendeen," I said disconsolately in an aside so Mo could not hear, "a pot-bellied stove is not my idea of central-heating. The kids in the back of the room will become frozen stalagmites while the kids up front here will resemble grilled hot-dogs. And," I added, "what about me...with...with my frozen front facing the children and my baked backside behind..." I found it necessary to be blunt.

"This won't be forever," Mr. Herendeen consoled. "Just a few days. Believe you me, kid, this town is goin' to do somethin' about Sesqui now...even if we—we have to force 'em to. Mrs. Davis and I and Mr. Jackson and Mrs. Jackson and her committee—and plenty of other people—we're all organizin'. Don't you worry," and he was gone.

But he did leave Old Mo to look after the fire. A built-in custodian-fireman-caretaker! Sesqui was coming of age.

Mrs. Davis, however, sensing for herself the abject bone-cold, low, low temperature of Sesqui, had mercy on me and on the children and informed me that she had an idea that would really turn our little school into "another Miami beach," she said.

"Just you wait," she concluded, jumping from Sesqui to her little side porch with one sporadic leap.

The idea of being parked this close to the Davis residence was of course to facilitate quick use of Mr. & Mrs. Davis' powder room facilities. Yes—at least—this was an improvement from Sesqui's previous position on the Centennial lawn, even though it was true—the drawbacks to this new arrangement were rapidly multiplying.

"Small wonder these kids don't grow up hating the sight of a persimmon," I mused, thinking of all those petulantly protected blue-ribbon winners.

"Hope the ashes don't mark up your carpet," commented Mo as he added more kindling wood. "Brought a porcelain coffee pot, too," he said to himself and to me. "I'll be perkin' some soon for ye," he added. Things were cozily shaping up.

And then the children began dribbling over from across the street. They were forlorn-looking waifs who, by luck or by chance, happened to find their port in the storm.

"What're we doin' over here?" Justin wanted to know.

"How'd they move it?" Henry Burnett asked, his big eyes puzzled.

"Who is 'they'?" I asked, curiously, thinking that I really hadn't been told who had moved Sesqui. It could have been Mr. Herendeen's crew or it could have been other G.O.T. men. It could even have been the men from Newton's Beanery...or perhaps Mrs. Davis hired professionals for the job herself.

But whoever it was hadn't had too much trouble. Sesqui was basically a portable trailer-classroom. She rested on no permanent foundation. She had, in fact, retained her original tires. She could easily have been just rolled over and...

"Wh...wh...wh..?." said the man from the doorway.

"Wh...wh...wh..." I tried to get started, but Mrs. Davis, back with her extensions and floor lamps interrupted:

"We've taken things into our own hands," she said decisively to Mr. Birly. "There are plenty of us who are plumb sick and tired of going through all that agony of collectin' all of $1,632, and then havin' the School Board squander it on snow plows!"

"I...I...take it," Mr. Birly began again, sizing things up, "you were outvoted."

"That I was," Mrs. Davis answered. "And snow," she added, with her nose in the air, "is not a permanent fixture. It melts, you know."

"Where do you want this, honey?" she turned to me with a tall lamp in her hand.

"Wh...wh...wha..." Mr. Birly began again.

"Mr. Birly," I said, resignedly to him, "I don't really know how we got over here. I just know that we're here. But we've got lights now and Old Mo there is trying to heat the place up. I'll be willing to teach for a while under these conditions as long as it's healthy enough for the children," I added. "If you think..."

"You *do* have a bathroom now," Mr. Birly interrupted, noting the short distance from Sesqui to Mrs. Davis's house. He shook his head. "I can't spare my custodians from their Centennial duties, however,—to remove all that toilet paper from the trees," he added, looking out of one of the windows.

"That's quite all right," I answered. "It's not bothering us."

"But it will scare the birds," put in Justin who shouldn't have been listening.

"I have a patrol boy out there directing the children across the street," Mr. Birly commented, shrugging his shoulders listlessly. Then, suddenly he was wrung with the helplessness of the situation:

"I don't like this, Miss Morrow," he said quietly. "I don't like you over here. And me 'way over there. What kind of a Principal can I be—to Sesqui—and to you, under these conditions?"

"Well, she's stayin'," interrupted Mrs. Davis, who came by on the last remark, "unless you want to roll her back over by yourself." Mrs. Davis was heartless.

"She's got somethin' over here, now," Mrs. Davis went on. "A good sound toilet. Two good sound toilets. Conveniences like she's never had..."

"Do you have a bath-tub?" Justin interrupted.

It was Mr. Jackson then who burst through the door with a whole herd of Sesqui-ites,—laughing, jeering, screeching, shoving.

"Do these belong to you, Miss Morrow?" he asked, smiling jovially.

"Now, now..." Mr. Birly began...

"OUCH! I got burned!" screamed Clifford, drawing his hand back from the black-bellied stove. Clifford was one to penetrate the environment immediately.

"Look!" declared Mary Jane, "we can put our wet mittens on these lamps to dry. Wow! They're hot, too!"

"No, no, no, no..." Mrs. Davis started to say.

About this time Robert Jackson had an announcement:

"Yikes! The bathroom upstairs—over in the house—has pink toilet paper and the one downstairs has polka dots! Yikes!"

"Robert!" Mr. Jackson said in alarm.

"And there are two bedrooms up and one down, Mrs. Davis," Robert turned to her suddenly, addressing her:

"Your bacon looks like it's done on top of the stove in the kitchen."

Mrs. Davis departed hurriedly—but she returned seconds later with Unita in tow.

"How'd I know Mr. Davis was in there takin' a shower?" she looked to me for compassion. Mrs. Davis left again.

"Aren't all these wires—lying about like this—" I thought it necessary to point out, "aren't they dangerous?" I asked Mr. Birly.

"No'm," Old Mo interrupted, "they're not so dangerous. If the floor was wet now. But," he added, "I'm goin' to trim all the wires that's hangin' around outside—so's no one gets hurt." And he whipped out those guillotine scissors he had used to cut Clifford's hair!

"My barber!" Clifford shouted from across the room. "It's the barber! I know you," he added, addressing Mo, "my mother's lookin' for you. She don't believe you're for real."

"I'd know your head anywheres," Old Mo replied to Clifford, nodding his head. "It's small. Real small."

Clifford's head in reality was perfectly normal. But, with his haircut growing out somewhat, it still resembled a muskmelon disguised as a coconut.

"Children! Children!" I called the class to order. "Let's get to our seats." For all of Sesqui's moving about, the desks somehow still retained their normal positions.

"I'm looking into this entire situation," Mr. Birly assured me and then stomped out.

"I shall return," he called over his shoulder.

"Can he bring marshmallows this afternoon?" Mary Jane wanted to know. "To roast?"

"Leave your coats on children," I cautioned, "until it warms up in here."

"This is fun," Sandy commented, but then she asked suddenly: "Oh-h-h-h-h-h-h-h do you think the cocoons froze during the night?"

"May I leave the room?" Justin interrupted.

"Is this absolutely necessary?" I wanted to know.

"Justin," I admonished, "be sure to come right back."

"Sure will," he replied, disappearing into Mrs. Davis' house almost as soon as he had departed from Sesqui.

How to keep order under such bizarre circumstances? The routine had been upset. It would require Herculean efforts on my part to even maintain a semblance of order under these conditions.

The reading circle convened finally around the pot-bellied stove, but then the rest of the class, working at their desks, complained that we were cutting the warmth off.

Justin ambled back now with currant jelly smeared all over his mouth, giving evidence that Mrs. Davis was now intent on fraternization which did not help discipline one iota. Now, when this new turn of events became known there would be a mass movement to be excused. So many disrupting influences!

At milk time, when I discovered that no delivery had been made, I sent Old Mo across the street to see what had happened. Mr. Birly subsequently directed him to Sesqui's former "spot" where the milkman had not only left the specified number of cartons—now frozen—but left a note as well:

> "You've flown the coop?" the note began. "Or is it the coop that has flown. Well, whatever. In case you'll be coming back here is your milk. You never said you was quittin' my service."
>
> Your Milkman

It was through the efforts of Mrs. Davis that the milk returned from ice to its liquid state in a matter of moments. It was Mrs. Davis' ingenious plan to keep us all warm. She merely, in a matter of fifteen minutes, hooked up an assortment of sun-lamps gathered from the immediate neighborhood—at each Sesqui window. Sesqui's wall thermometer, therefore, zoomed skyward in seconds, as the warm, warm, lamps poured their 'all' onto Sesqui.

But again I asked the question: "Was this altogether safe?"

And the questions:

"Wasn't there something about ultra-violet rays or something?"

"Wasn't it getting too warm—too quickly?" I asked this last, slipping out of the jacket to my suit.

When Mary Jane shed her coat, then her sweater, and finally her overblouse, however, I was convinced.

And Old Mo was wiping his brow!

"Do ye think I put too much coal on the fire?" he came over to my desk. "I never did see such a powerful pot-belly," he declared appreciatively.

"I wish I had worn a cool cotton," I answered him.

"Mo," I thought I should take precautions, "why don't you run over and tell Mrs. Davis that it's getting too hot in here. Tell her to disconnect the lamps at least for a while."

What was really beginning to worry me was the fact that no one had to be excused in the last half hour. "Do you suppose they're dehydrated?" I asked myself.

Mo left.

"Wow!" Clifford complained, "I'm hot."

"I know," I said simply. "But I hate to open the door. We might catch cold with a sudden draft...But, then, perhaps I'd better," I was talking to myself aloud.

"Oh, please don't open the door, Miss Morrow!" Sandy pleaded in hushed tones. "Look!"

I looked where she pointed—to the science table.

"Our cocoons are hatching!" Sandy exclaimed, breathlessly.

It was so. One Cecropia Moth was already halfway up the wall—its wings fragile as wet tissue paper.

Another Polyphemus chrysalis was empty!

Where was this moth?

A Tiger Swallowtail butterfly was posing motionless beside a yet unhatched Cecropia pupa.

"But, Miss Morrow," Sandy was pleading, "where will they go?"

Crumpled wings were slowly stiffening into gorgeous displays of brilliant color. Magnificent!

Never Pluck a Persimmon

"The snow is all over—everywhere," Sandy was still concerned. "What will the moths eat?"

"Oh, yes," I came back to the immediate problem. Just as I was certain I would burst out of my underwear if those sun lamps didn't soon let up...the lights were suddenly turned off. Mo had made his point!

"Sandy," I said gently to my sensitive one, "more often than not the moths—when they leave the cocoon—have no mouth at all anyway."

"No mouths?" Justin was horrified.

"Then they can't eat or drink," Robert Jackson came to the conclusion.

"That's correct," I answered. "They do not eat or drink. They're not supposed to. They only mate and lay their eggs. Then they die."

"They die hungry," Sandy said quietly, fighting tears.

"But happy," put in Mary Jane, completely reconciled to the ways-of-the-world.

"Oh-h-h-h-h that's awful!" Sandy sobbed, and I reached out my arms to her.

"Sandy," I consoled, "we can help the moths. We can keep the door closed so that they will mate and lay their eggs right here in Sesqui. Then," I continued, knowing the improbability of it all, "perhaps, if all goes well, we will have their little baby caterpillars in a while..."

"And then we could mount the dead moths," put in Justin tactlessly.

The tears started fresh.

"But," I continued hopefully, wiping Sandy's cheeks with a paper tissue, "about the butterflies now. They sip nectar. They have mouths. They can eat. Perhaps Mrs. Davis will let us have some of her flowers to put here in Sesqui so that..." and here I had to stop...

The missing Polyphemus moth with its large eye-shaped markings on its hind wings was looking at me, fore and aft, from a most likely perch—atop Clifford's new haircut! I had to admit it. The addition was an improvement.

XXVI

THE SIDES ARE DRAWN

That very night the Greentree Times demanded in big, black letters:

"SESQUI, COME BACK!"

and then listed all the reasons why it was imperative for Sesqui to return to Centennial.

"What does this do to the Principal, Mr. Birly?" the article asked. "It tears him asunder," the paper answered. "It makes him neither here nor there!"

Another item about the same subject quoted Mr. Clay of the School Board as saying:

"A house divided against itself cannot stand!" and Mr. Webster, also of the Board, declaring:

"The voice of reason is stilled!" and then he went on to say that Sesqui could eventually be forced to return if the Board would decide to cut off Sesqui's utilities and money allocations...

"Humph," I thought, "the utilities had already been cut off—torn up, literally,...but then we did have Mrs. Davis' lovely facilities.

To prevent the third graders from wandering about the Davis household at random Mo and I devised a system whereby when a child wanted to go to the restroom we would slip a carefully-measured string about his or her waist, one that would allow the child to reach only the bathroom downstairs. This prevented further damage to Mr. Davis' tools in the basement and to Mrs. Davis' oil paintings in the attic. If the string,which was attached to the side of my desk snapped suddenly, well, then, Mo would take off to catch the culprit.

By the third day of all this, however, I could see that Mr. Davis' nerves were beginning to fray. The kids were hard enough to cope with but Mo barging in and out of every cranny, and at such odd times, in the Davis household was a little bit much.

On the fourth day Mrs. Davis herself asked us quietly to cut the string once and for all and let the kids roam wherever they so desired. This, however, meant that both Mr. & Mrs. Davis had to be in constant surveillance—what with their weekly groceries and all out in the open on the kitchen shelves. The refrigerator could be roped and knotted without too much trouble, but the kitchen shelves presented spread-out problems of their own.

I had noticed, also, that Mrs. Davis was not as vociferous in her demands by the end of the fourth day.

"We rally as one!" she had been quoted as saying the first day, emphasizing the unity behind the Cause.

The second day she had referred to the Satellite School as:

"The Glorious Sovereign State of Sesqui!"

By the third day, however, although pointing out that those in favor of getting Sesqui connected did have dynamic leadership, she also called attention to the fact that number-wise the Sesqui-ites were a minority.

"Sesqui has the will," she declared dramatically, "but Centennial has the means!"

By the fourth evening, however, she was suggesting arbitration:

"Sesqui's liberties could be acquired if an historic conference could be arranged..."

Mr. Birly, it can be said in all honesty, did everything in his power to preserve the peace. He ran back and forth between Sesqui and Centennial like a basketball player going from one basket to the other and frustratingly, never scoring. But, as in any situation anywhere, some good did come from the very uniqueness of having such incongruities as Mr. Birly and Old Mo thrown together.

"Wh...wh...wha," Mr. Birly said to Mo one day, about to ask him some questions.

"Wa-Wa!" Mo said. "Give me two dollars and I'll put it on Wa-Wa for you in the fifth."

And, Mr. Birly, utterly confused and thinking that Sesqui needed some new trivia to keep irate parents quiet, handed over the $2.00. Of course, when Wa-Wa won, well, Mr. Birly and Old Mo became the best of friends.

The fact that Sesqui was the small one—compared to Centennial—did not deter the President of the School Board from crying out over the Greentree radio on the 6:15 "Interpreting the News" program:

"Sesqui's smallness, Sesqui's maneuverability, this, is Sesqui's strength. Remember, it was the Greeks against the powerful Persians—the first Queen Elizabeth against Philip II—tiny Netherlands against Spain,

Frederick the Great in the eighteenth century against the combined powers of Europe—and, "he added for emphasis, "anemic America in 1776 against Gargantuan Great Britain. Now," he added dramatically, "it is wee Sesqui against mighty Centennial. The sides are drawn!"

How long Sesqui could have held out is not exactly known. But what is known is that on the fifth day both of the Davis' toilets backed up, perhaps from the increased usage, presenting an additional problem.

Five plumbers, after much deliberation, decided that the Davis lawn would have to be dug up, necessitating the moving of Sesqui. A nearby gasoline station, hearing of Sesqui's plight, offered its facilities but then re-nigged, fearing a loss of business for flaunting its politics. No one else offered refuge to Sesqui. Sesqui had no alternative but to go home to Centennial. But Mrs. Davis, in one last lunge, stated in the Greentree Times:

"Proudly Sesqui returns to the soil she so reluctantly left behind—just five short days ago. But she returns with her head held high. Instead of occupying her former site, however, thirty feet away from Centennial, she will be placed flat smack close to the Mother School until that time when the School Board returns the $1,632.00 which rightfully belongs to Sesqui—to begin proceedings to get Sesqui connected."

And that very night Sesqui was rolled back over—across the street—to be placed near Centennial again, but this time, as Mrs. Davis predicted, smack square in the middle of the prize persimmon trees, near Centennial. "Glad to have you back!" Mr. Birly greeted me the next morning, his avant-garde eyes alive with the joy that was in him. He really looked as though he meant it. "I'm glad to be back!" I answered, smiling. "The Electric Company will be here any minute to connect you," Mr. Birly informed. "Fine," I answered. "And," he continued, "we'll soon see to it that you can get rid of that stove," he nodded to the obsolete fixture. "Where's Mo?" he asked, looking around. "I haven't seen him yet this morning," I answered. "Well, when he comes in tell him I'd like to have a haircut," he said, going out the door. "Was Mr. Birly serious?" I didn't know. When Old Mo did appear he had a bit of advice for me: "Miss Morrow, there's only one thing about your teaching I think is not right," he began apologetically. "But I'm goin' to speak out so's you can correct it."

"Yes, Mo," I was certainly open to suggestions at this point.

Never Pluck a Persimmon

"Well," Mo continued, apparently re-living his past, "I think that for a one-room schoolhouse you spend an awful lot of time—too much time," he added thoughtfully, "on third grade!" There, it was out!

"Why thank you, Mo," I said understandingly. "I'm glad you told me that. I'll try to do something about it." And then I told him about the haircut Mr. Birly wanted.

"I'll have to find my scissors first," Mo said rather impulsively. Was it my imagination or was Mo already starting to shake?

It was hours later that the fruit of many labors became common knowledge in Greentree. A few minutes past the dismissal hour, after the last gleeful child's voice had echoed across the spacious Centennial stretch of ground—I could suddenly see two figures looming on the horizon, heading Sesqui's way. They were both struggling under the weight of an enormous carton. One, one was Mo, yes, but the other? Why it was Mr. Birly, looking as though he had investigated trouble in his power mower—with his head!

I swung open the door and the audible pantings of the two men as they labored under their burden made steamy-clouds in the almost-zero atmosphere.

"Supplies?" I called to them.

Neither could answer. They hadn't the breath. Carefully they manipulated their way into Sesqui, edging this way and then that way to get through the door.

Mr. Birly still did not speak. With an incomprehensible shake of his head—which now resembled a coconut disguised as a muskmelon, he simply dug into his pocket to retrieve a small piece of white paper.

It was a note of some kind. With a gesture Mr. Birly indicated that I should read the contents therein.

Slowly, hardly trusting what my eyes told me, I read:

Dear Mr. Birly,

    The County Police told us people here how 16 strangers came into your town and stole the clothes right off the backs of your men citizens.

    We, the Citizens Committee of Tintown, U.S.A. therefore organized and collected a few things which we are certain will be of great use now to the men of Greentree, U.S.A.

Our deepest sympathy,
The Tintown, U.S.A.
Citizens' Committee

"Wh...wh...wh...," Mr. Birly was starting to say.

XXVII

THE WET SPRING

But after all, what could be said?

Thinking that if the contents of the box were ever revealed then all future Clothing Drives in the Greentree Schools would be forever doomed, Mr. Birly, with my approval and blessing, decided to quietly bestow upon Mo, the clothing. If Mo could not-use everything himself, well, there would always be those who might possibly lose their shirts in the room behind Mo's Barber Shop...

But just to look at Mr. Birly with his ridiculous new haircut—it was evident he had gone the full circle of his winning streak.

"Wh...wh...wh..." he started to say to Mo.

"You want Wa-Wa again?" Old Mo preempted. "He's not running."

"No," Mr. Birly stated flatly. "I'm finished gambling. It's not principal-like," he finished.

"Mr. Birly was no doubt secretly worried about leaving Mo's premises in a pair of Tintown trousers himself," I concluded.

And the days went by and gradually the snow melted but Sesqui remained unconnected.

For all the dear old Greentree ladies who were deeply concerned about the persimmon trees taking a beating from the third graders—Sesqui remained where she had been temporarily placed—in the midst of the trees in the center of a low spot. And while the Board deliberated and tried to scrounge up the money to see about paying the plumbers and contractor and arriving at something definite—and while people still argued the pros and cons of doing so—Sesqui, as a great thaw set in, sank deeper and deeper into the mud!

And the spring rains came, one after the other, and the whole world became a wet kind of squishiness! And as the unrelenting precipitation proceeded, shower by shower, umbrella by umbrella, and day after day, the lemony-beige rug slowly evolved into a tanny-tawny sand shade and from the tanny-tawny sand shade it finally changed to a muddy, mud-turtle brown where it stayed.

"We could use a draw-bridge," Justin said, commenting on the large quantity of water immediately surrounding Sesqui herself.

"We can't go out for recess," I told the children who were struggling with boots to go to the lavatory over in Centennial, "it's too wet!"

"So," I continued, "we'll stay inside and Miss Morrow will play some records. Then perhaps we'll do some marching—for exercise," I added enthusiastically.

"Miss Morrow," Clifford began, "I have some goldfish at home. I could put them in that big puddle outside. It's deep enough."

"No," I said to Clifford. "Don't bring your goldfish." It was bad enough we still hadn't found his Mother's gallstones let alone...

Over at Centennial things seemed normal enough. We waited until the second grades completed their monopoly of the fountains and then we waited again at the toilets—with the exception of Robert Jackson who charged full speed ahead of everyone, at my suggestion.

By the time we had completed our "johning" a crash of thunder told us there was yet more rain to come. The heavens subsequently opened to one pelting, pummelling, pouring deluge just as we arrived at the Centennial door on our way back to Sesqui. And so we waited again for a slackening pace before braving the cruel, wet world that existed between Sesqui and Centennial.

"Boys and girls," I started, once inside Sesqui's dry walls, "because we had to take so long this morning over at Centennial, perhaps we had better skip our marching today."

"But you promised," retorted Justin.

"Indian-giver," said Henry disgusted.

"All right. All right," I complied, "but you'll have to work at your arithmetic extra-hard now to make up the time."

Then I added:

"Fifteen minutes before dismissal time, then, we'll devote to marching." And it was settled.

And the papers and pencils were brought out anew as the boys and girls completed their math assignments. And outside, the rains continued.

"What if Sesqui becomes completely surrounded by all this water?" I thought worriedly. "What if we become marooned out here in this mud-hole? It would be like being shipwrecked on a lonely island—with twenty jumping Fridays!"

If all these imaginings were realities, would Mr. Birly fly in my art supplies and gum erasers by helicopter? And would the Music Supervisor swim the "channel" to bestow a little culture on us? Could the children go to the Centennial lavatories via rubber raft? Would wild ducks congregate in and about and on Sesqui and increase and multiply and form a wet version of a St. Mark's Square? Or a sanctuary of a sort?

"Will the first row turn in the arithmetic paper now?" I said in a directive tone, coming back to reality, "time is up."

I held my hands out for the papers but the child who brought them to me seemed to stagger for balance. And why did I suddenly experience a slight sensation of dizziness? Was the strain of teaching taking its toll?

"The second row, now," I continued, still puzzled by the funny feeling.

"May I put the record on now—for the marching?" leader Mary Jane wanted to know.

"Yes," I agreed, as I finished collecting the remainder of the arithmetic papers.

"Go to your marching places now," I said and the entire class moved to the south end of Sesqui. Everything was normal. What was wrong with me?

And the record began:

"THE GRAND OLD DUKE OF YORK." the narrator said in his deep, authoritative voice.

"HE HAD 10,000 MEN!"

The boys and girls in five straight lines, began stamping their feet in unison as I clapped out the rhythm for them.

They marched! Oh, how they marched! Their knees touched their chins!

Now the entire class was on the northern end. Then, in unison, they marched back to the south.

"HE MARCHED THEM UP TO THE TOP OF THE HILL
AND HE MARCHED THEM DOWN AGAIN."

The marchers then stopped and turned and began again in the reverse direction:

"AND WHEN THEY WERE UP THEY WERE UP.
(Reverse again)
AND WHEN THEY WERE DOWN THEY WERE DOWN.
(Reverse again)
AND WHEN THEY WERE ONLY HALFWAY UP THEY WERE NEITHER UP NOR DOWN."

"AGAIN," called the voice from the record and the marching continued with ever increased enthusiasm.

The entire Class so enjoyed the marching. The boys and girls all tried to outdo one another. They laughed and gestured to one another and followed along with the narrator. They marched. From the South to the North. From the North to the South, and the man on the record set their pace:

"THE GRAND OLD DUKE OF YORK
HE HAD TEN THOUSAND MEN.
HE MARCHED THEM UP TO THE TOP OF THE HILL
AND HE MARCHED THEM DOWN..."

At the "down" Sesqui suddenly lurched, trembled a little, and then hiccoughed, throwing everyone off balance!

I staggered and then grabbed my desk and held on for dear life. But the lurching subsided suddenly into a quiet kind of limpid ooziness! Sesqui rose and fell in soft, gentle, rocking motions.

There was no question about it.

"Good Lord!"

Sesqui was floating!

Within seconds Sesqui had been transformed into a streamlined Noah's Ark! "There were two sea shells on the science table," I thought wildly, "two geraniums on the window sills, two birds' nests, two stuffed pheasants, and two boxes of rocks in all." Sesqui had all the necessary qualifications—two of each kind of thing.

The boys and girls giggled and squealed nervously. None was hurt that I could see.

"Miss Morrow," Henry Burnett said apprehensively, "are we moving?"

"Yes," Robert Jackson answered, in a high nervous voice.

The lights blinked and reblinked in nervous twitches.

I pulled myself to my feet and then staggered to the nearest window to see if I could see Mr. Birly or a bird or anything with dry land in its beak.

But the only "bird" in evidence was a lone mother waiting under an umbrella for her child. I couldn't see her face but when she suddenly started waving the umbrella up and down in frantic, jerky movements I took it that she was protesting the "Sailing Sesqui."

The H.M.S. Sesqui slurped to the outer rim of the puddle—to the west—and then buoyed back to the middle again. There Sesqui bided her time, rising and falling in little titilating gestures.

"Miss Morrow," it was Clifford, "how will we get home for our lunches?"

"Class," I said as calmly as I could, "we really have nothing to worry about. The water rose underneath Sesqui—and it lifted us up a little bit."

"Will we get to the ocean?" Henry wanted to know.

"I can't swim," Mary Jane lamented.

"There is nothing to worry about. We'll just wait a few minutes to see if Mr. Birly won't put some wooden planks out for us—or provide us with something to step on, to go home for our lunches." I was only in reality worried about the electricity, with possible wire snappings, etc., and fallen wires possibly hidden in the water...

When we reached the eastern-most point of the puddle I estimated we had traveled a good ten feet from the spot where Sesqui had broken loose from her moorings. Then, as suddenly as we had embarked, we disembarked! With a shivering shudder Sesqui ran dead into a Mt. Ararat, in reality a six inch grassy sand bar, which sent the youngsters scrambling again.

Never Pluck a Persimmon

But then the lights flickered again and then came on strong, and the children smiled and started putting on coats and boots, convinced that this time, for sure, they would be going home for lunch.

"Boy! That was fun!" Mary Jane sighed.

"And scary," Clifford said.

"Miss Morrow," Justin reported, looking out a window, "there are three firetrucks coming this way—across the grass!"

Blaring sirens authenticated this latest pronouncement!

The children jumped with excitement and ran to the windows.

"Whee-ee-ee-ee-ee! We're being surrounded!" called Robert Jackson.

I stared in utter disbelief as I made out Mr. Birly in his new haircut—in Truck Number One!

And, what a record the third-graders set!

In less than ten seconds ladders were extended over and across the puddle to Sesqui's windows and the giddy, gleeful third-graders evacuated their School in one mad, merry rush while a Greentree Times' photographer popped his flash-bulbs in accompaniment.

True to tradition it was the Captain who stayed with the ship 'til the last little pair o' buttocks went over and down the last ladder.

"Miss Morrow," said Mr. Birly, visibly shaken, and taking my hand to assist me over the ladder, "as God is my Judge, I'm going to get you connected!"

As I groped for my footing on the almost horizontal ladder I noticed three firemen on Truck No. 1 directly below watching my every move., as well as Mr. Birly's.

"Oh, Miss Morrow," Mr. Birly was saying, commenting on my plight of the moment, "you deserve a medal for this inconvenience, or combat pay, or whatever..."

XXVIII

THE SCHOOL BOARD RESOLVES...

That evening the Greentree Times, in addition to carrying the pictures of Sesqui floating on the Centennial lawn, presented several indignant articles about Sesqui's continuing plight in general.

"What are the citizens of Greentree waiting for?" asked one of the pieces. "The School Board continues to place money above justice and convenience," commented the other.

Even Mrs. Puternaugh, Greentree's No. 1 Substitute Teacher, wrote a letter to the Editor wherein she deplored Sesqui's primitive condition:

"Mine eyes have seen," she declared, having truly been an eye-witness, and her epistle ended on a plaintive tone:

"Why must Sesqui's Rights continue being a Lost Cause?" she asked.

"And why did it?" I asked myself after I had read what she had said. Was there to be no arbitration board—no Summit confrontations—no, no...anything? Just leave things as they are, the School Board seemed to be saying in their silence, leave Sesqui parked where she is—leave her what she is—an old, stick-in-the-mud. "How long," I asked myself, "must things go along this way?" How many more times would we have to don all those coats and boots and hats and gloves to go to Centennial at lavatory time? But what was the use? What kind of impact can a minute gnat make against a mighty elephant?

And, because it was already spring, I speculated, was the Board now considering that it was far too late to bother installing anything this year? Were they going to wait 'til next year—'til simmons fall again—to do something? And in the meantime...

But the next day the sun shone and all was well. And then after school I glanced out the nearest Sesqui window to behold the glorious late afternoon sun which was penetrating every slumbering blade of grass within reach.. except of course for the ones Sesqui was strangulating.

"Miss Morrow!" a voice said from Sesqui's doorway. "May we come in?" It was Mrs. Davis!

"Certainly," I said, and remembering her previous experience with the third-graders I added, "it's safe. They've gone home for the day!"

Never Pluck a Persimmon

As I reached the entrance way to open the screen door which I had hooked when the children left, I noted almost the entire Greentree School Board standing there!

"Well," I exclaimed, surprised, "how are you all?" I addressed them all at once, the Messrs. Calhoun Jones, Webster, Clay, and of course, Mrs. Davis.

"Come in. Come in," I said nervously. "Such a delegation!" I said to myself, wondering whatever...

The four of them entered Sesqui and stood stiffly to the one side, as though waiting to view the body.

"Is...is there anything I can do for you?" I asked hesitantly, overwhelmed that such a contingent should call on me...

"Yes," Mrs. Davis answered, "you can listen to our report—before it is published in the newspaper tonight. We've just come from Mr. Birly's office where we read him the report...and he said," Mrs. Davis continued, "that we should come directly over to you and let you hear it—before the newspapers publish it," she repeated.

"There was no joy in Mudville," I recited to myself.

"You'd better sit down," Mr. Clay ceremoniously directed me to a small chair in the reading circle. Mr. Webster then cleared his throat and perched precariously on the one next to me while Mrs. Davis remained standing like a Swiss guard, or whatever, *sans* hat...

It was Mr. Clay, then, who dragged over the Teacher's chair, coughed self-consciously into his handkerchief, and began intoning:

> Whereas the pre-Spring pre-registration and also the Spring registration for the Centennial School District discloses that the projected enrollment at Centennial for the School Year '01-02 is down considerably, (the projected enrollment figures being in the neighborhood of 590 compared to the 640 students now attending Centennial); it is therefore the conclusion of the Board that Sesqui of Centennial, [Mr. Clay never alternated from the subliminal monotone] the portable classroom that has been in use there, will not be needed for the school year '01-02.

Mr. Clay continued, never lifting his eyes:

Virginia Morrow Black

The Spring Registration figures for Harrison School, however, on the west side of Greentree show a projected enrollment increase of some fifty pupils. It is therefore the decision of the Board that Sesqui of Centennial be moved to the West side of town to become a part of Harrison School to alleviate the overcrowding in that building!

And here Mr. Clay looked up!

"Am I supposed to say something?" my mind was rushing along, trying to grasp the full meaning of so many words!

"How can I say anything?" I thought, "I'm speechless!"

Sesqui-Centennial to become Sesqui-Harrison?

"Of course we realize this is a shock to you, my dear," put in Mrs. Davis, "but this is why the Board has taken so long...to connect Sesqui," she added.

"We don't connect fly-by-nights," Mr. Webster commented tactlessly.

"However," Mr. Clay was saying, "Mr Birly is perfectly satisfied with your work here. And we'd like it very much if you would go with Sesqui—to Harrison. We'd see to it that you'd get the third-grade there," he assured, "and Sesqui would be parked smack beside Harrison!" he smiled.

"They have no persimmon trees there," Mrs. Davis put in.

"Mr. Birly!" I thought, "satisfied with my work?" That was something. I had never been told this.

But there was unfinished business at Sesqui.

What about all those thieves that had taken all those wallets? What about my darling youngsters? What about their good parents?...

And Harrison...another third grade...a new principal...new boys and girls...a different part of town...but, still—and the thought cheered me somehow, "I'd still have Sesqui!"

I turned to face my visitors squarely:

"I'd be happy to go with Sesqui," I said, sure of myself now. "I'm buying a car and the west-side isn't very far. I can probably even remain with Mrs. Decklebaum." I found myself thinking out loud.

"Fine," Mr. Webster said, smiling and reaching for his hat.

"Fine," Mr. Clay said, folding up his papers.

"Fine," Mrs. Davis said, clasping my hand.

"Fine," Mr. Calhoun Jones said, getting to his feet.

And there were more hand-clasps and the delegation left, their business accomplished.

As I watched them tip-toeing to their cars, ever so solicitous to step only in the Proper Places just in case a little ol' slip of a 'simmon might be poking through in the warm sunshine now, I had a thought:

It was as it should be.

Sesqui was a separate entity in herself—a flexible unit in a flexible society. She had never been Centennial. She would never be Harrison. She was as free as the air, and now she was moving on...

With a flair for independence, her constant idealistic strivings, with her completely blithe little spirit—it was fitting and proper that she should remain free and unconnected...It was as it should be.

And the Greentree Times, commenting on the School Board's decision that night, complimented them on their wisdom, and then, to placate any dissenting opinion or any ruffled feelings, finished its piece thus:

> With malice toward none with charity for all, with firmness in the right as God gives us to see the right—let us strive on to finish the work we are in—to bind up our wounds—to do all which may achieve and cherish a just and a lasting peace among ourselves and with all mankind.

"And, as Sandy would say," I thought, putting the paper aside, "God bless us, every one!"

ABOUT THE AUTHOR

Virginia Morrow Black, with twenty-four years experience teaching in Hoosier elementary and secondary schools, writes about what she knows best,- teaching children and young adults in Indiana schools.

Her latest book, *NEVER PLUCK A PERSIMMON*, is one such example, although it is a fictionalized account of teaching a third grade class in a portable classroom in the make-believe town of Greentree, Indiana.

A graduate of Seton Hill College, Pennsylvania, Mrs. Black hails from Glassport, PA. (17 miles from Pittsburgh) but considers herself a Hoosier since she has lived in South Bend, Indiana since 1951.

Her four children, all now parents themselves, hail from Wisconsin and Maryland as well as from Indiana. Twelve grandchildren, one of whom is handicapped, occupy much of her time. Anthony R. Black, a Professor of European history at St. Mary's College, Notre Dame, Indiana, Mrs. Black's husband of 47 years, died in 1997.

Her writing credits include four plays (all comedies) published in 1989-1990. A previous book, *TACKLING NOTRE DAME*, a humorous account of how Mrs. Black earned a PhT degree (Put him Through) while her husband earned a Ph. D. in history, was published in 1985 and is still selling in college bookstores.

Virginia Morrow Black's biography can be found in Who's Who of American Women as well as in Who's Who in America. She lives in an apartment in South Bend, having recently sold her home of thirty years.

Printed in the United States
5266